US Commanders of World War II (1)

Army & USAAF

J. Arnold & R. Hargis • Illustrated by Darko Pavlovic

First published in Great Britain in 2002 by Osprey Publishing,
Elms Court, Chapel Way, Botley, Oxford OX2 9LP, United Kingdom.
Email: info@ospreypublishing.com

ISBN 1 84176 474 4

CONSULTANT EDITOR: MARTIN WINDROW

Editor: Anita Hitchings
Design: Alan Hamp
Biographies and photo captions: James R Arnold & Roberta Wiener
Colour plate references and commentaries: Robert Hargis & Starr Sinton
Index by Alan Rutter

Originated by The Electronic Page Company, Cwmbran, UK
Printed in China through World Print Ltd.

02 03 04 05 06   10 9 8 7 6 5 4 3 2 1

FOR A CATALOG OF ALL BOOKS PUBLISHED BY
OSPREY MILITARY AND AVIATION PLEASE CONTACT:

Osprey Direct USA, c/o MBI Publishing, P.O. Box 1,
729 Prospect Ave, Osceola, WI 54020, USA
E-mail: **info@ospreydirectusa.com**

Osprey Direct UK, P.O. Box 140,
Wellingborough, Northants, NN8 2FA, UK
E-mail: **info@ospreydirect.co.uk**

www.ospreypublishing.com

Artist's note

Readers may care to note that the original paintings from which the
color plates in this book were prepared are available for private sale.
All reproduction copyright whatsoever is retained by the Publishers.
All enquiries should be addressed to:

Darko Pavlovic, Modecova 3, Zagreb, 10090, Croatia

The Publishers regret that they can enter into no correspondence
upon this matter.

US COMMANDERS OF WORLD WAR II (1) ARMY AND USAAF

INTRODUCTION

THE CONSTITUTION OF THE UNITED STATES gave the president supreme control over all armed forces. Before and during World War Two, President Franklin D. Roosevelt served as president and commander-in-chief. A civilian Secretary of War controlled the War Department, and through it, the army. The War Department included three distinct army organizational groupings: chiefs of the arms (e.g. infantry, armor, field artillery); services (supply and administration); and general staff (planning).

When war began in September 1939, the US Army had a 190,000-man Regular Army, an air arm, a 200,000-man National Guard composed of civilian volunteers, and an Organized Reserve with a nucleus of reserve officers. It was quickly apparent that the army was far too small. In particular, it severely lacked professional officers. A rapid and enormous expansion began that saw regular army officers, who had been stuck among the ranks of the junior officers for years, vault into senior command levels.

The outbreak of global war, and the attendant need to cooperate with other nations, revealed the urgent necessity for a stronger civilian-military command structure and army-navy coordination. Consequently,

The Arcadia Conference from December 22, 1941 to January 14, 1942 contrasted a well-oiled British planning organization with a fragmented American system. Inspired by the British, the Americans created the Joint Chiefs of Staff. From March 1942 on, its membership consisted of Admiral Ernest King (left), General George Marshall (left-rear), chairman Admiral William D. Leahy (right-rear), and General 'Hap' Arnold (right). Marshall and King were the dominant voices. (The George C. Marshall Research Library, Lexington, VA)

in February 1942, the Joint Chiefs of Staff (JCS) replaced the Joint Board as the highest military authority. Among the four members of the JCS were Army Chief of Staff, George Marshall, and the commanding general of the US Army Air Forces, Lieutenant-General Henry Arnold. The JCS both controlled the nation's armed forces and advised the president on everything from strategy to industrial policy.

In March 1942, the old General Headquarters was replaced by three separate but equal organizations. Lieutenant-General Lesley McNair's Army Ground Forces supervised training functions. The air arm, while remaining part of the army, acquired its own command structure. Lieutenant-General Brehon Somervell's Army Service Forces (originally called Services of Supply) took over logistics and procurement. These new organizations relieved Marshall and his general staff of much responsibility and allowed them to concentrate on operational strategy and planning. Marshall, in turn, reorganized and expanded the War Plans Division into an Operations Division that became the nerve center for all operations. Marshall used the Operations Division to supervise the theater commands and coordinate their logistical needs.

The army group, each with two or more armies, was the highest US Army organization operating in the field. The composition of each army group depended upon the vagaries of coalition warfare. Thus, Omar Bradley's 12th Army Group was almost entirely American, while Jacob Devers' 6th was half French, and Mark Clark's 15th was a diverse international force. The US Army organized 11 field armies during the war. Each army had at least two corps. During the war the army formed 26 new corps. Each corps typically had one armored and two infantry divisions, plus supporting arms and services. The US Army eventually expanded to 90 divisions. By the war's end this proved barely sufficient even though its strength, not including the Air Force, had risen to over six million men.

As with the ground forces, in September 1939, the Army Air Forces were minuscule in comparison to national needs. There were only 17 airbases in the United States. By 1943 this had grown to 345 main bases, 116 secondary bases, and 322 auxiliary fields. The wartime expansion saw a force of 20,196 with 2,470 mostly obsolete planes grow to almost 1.9 million men and women with 79,908 modern aircraft. Sixteen air forces were raised to carry out combat missions. Larger forces required higher command structures. In January 1944, the 8th and 15th Air Forces formed Carl Spaatz's Europe-based US Strategic Air Forces. In August 1944, George Kenney's Far East Air Forces was established to direct the operations of the 5th, 7th, and 13th Air Forces in the Pacific. To the delight of all air force leaders, the US Air Force finally became independent of the army in September 1947.

BIOGRAPHIES

US ARMY

George Catlett Marshall

Born in Uniontown, Pennsylvania in 1880, Marshall went south to attend the Virginia Military Institute. After his graduation in 1901, he received an infantry commission as a second lieutenant. Marshall achieved recognition during World War One through his brilliant staff service. By 1918, he had been named chief of operations for the US 1st Army in France. Marshall's next major step came in 1938 when he headed the War Plans Division of the Army General Staff and served as deputy chief of staff. In September 1939, he became army chief of staff.

Marshall enjoyed President Roosevelt's absolute confidence. Therefore, he had great influence at all of the major Allied wartime conferences. Although he possessed a fierce temper, he held it in check and adopted a practical approach to all problems. This, coupled with his lack of boastfulness, made for good relations with the British. Marshall hoped he would receive command of the Allied forces that would invade Europe. However, Roosevelt preferred him to remain in Washington, DC, where he would be available for close and frequent discussion. To his great credit, Marshall was able to prevent the president from meddling in military decision making. Marshall made another great contribution to the American war effort by his selection and assignment of senior officers. In addition, he made sure that generals who needed specific technical assistance received appropriate staff officers. Marshall shares with Admiral King the responsibility for failing to unify command in the Pacific. Pacific operations unwisely remained divided between the navy under Admiral Nimitz and the army under General MacArthur. The resultant two-prong advance against Japan gave the Japanese the opportunity to concentrate forces to defeat the widely separated American efforts. Fortunately, the Japanese failed to seize the chance. Because of Marshall's ability to provide grand strategic direction and to coordinate strategy with the Allies, Winston Churchill, who liked and admired him, bestowed upon him the honorific, "the organizer of victory."

Eisenhower (left) received a visit from George Marshall (right) in October 1944. (National Archives)

Marshall resigned from active service on November 20, 1945. President Truman quickly persuaded him to return to public service. After Marshall had held several diplomatic roles, in January 1947 Truman appointed him as Secretary of State. Marshall held this position until 1949, during which time he supervised the postwar reconstruction of western Europe, the famous Marshall Plan. Unjust attacks by the anti-communist zealot, Senator Joseph McCarthy, helped drive Marshall from public service in 1951. Two years later, Marshall became the first soldier to receive the Nobel Peace Prize. He died in 1959.

How Marshall might have fared as supreme field commander is unknown. In the view of his admirers, the fact that this position went to General Eisenhower denied Marshall his "rightful place in history." Still, no other American military figure had more influence upon the war. He was not a brilliant man. Rather, by sheer hard work and much common sense, Marshall earned Churchill's sobriquet.

General Lesley McNair was the single most important architect of American ground forces as they prepared for land warfare in Europe. He was efficient and decisive as well as highly opinionated. McNair self-confidently believed that he knew best what equipment ground forces required for combat. He emphasized mobility over combat power, a notion that was useful during the pursuit across France but was badly out of step with combat reality when American forces had to fight through fixed positions. (The George C. Marshall Research Library, Lexington, VA)

Lesley James McNair

Born in Verndale, Minnesota in 1883, Lesley "Whitney" McNair graduated from the US Military Academy at West Point with an artillery commission in 1904. Before World War One, McNair held various positions in the Ordnance Corps and went to Europe to study French artillery tactics. He participated in the 1914 expedition to Vera Cruz and served with Pershing during the Punitive Expedition in 1916. Major McNair served with the 1st Division in France in 1917. He gained a reputation as a very competent artillerist while working to develop techniques to accomplish the tactical "Holy Grail" of World War One: effective infantry-artillery cooperation. His talents earned him temporary promotion to brigadier-general, marking him as the youngest general officer in the American Expeditionary Force.

At the end of the war, he reverted to his permanent rank of major. He taught at the General Service School, completed the Army War College, and rose to command the Command and General Staff College at Fort Leavenworth. Between April 1939 and July 1940, he reformed the Command and General Staff College, making it "the crucial educational institution for senior American officers" in World War Two. McNair's next assignment was as chief of staff of Army General Headquarters in Washington, DC. Because of his staff and teaching duties during the interwar years, McNair influenced the development of American Army doctrine. However, he did not prove farsighted regarding tanks, since he saw them as mere mechanized cavalry, useful only for exploitation and pursuit. He believed that in the future, attacks would still hinge upon the traditional infantry-artillery team. McNair's pet project was the so-called tank destroyer. This ill-conceived program tried to unite mobility and gun power, at the expense of armored protection. The tank destroyers proved unsatisfactory in real combat. Worse, reliance upon them meant that designs for the standard American tanks, up to and including the M4 Sherman tank, were gravely flawed.

Promoted to the rank of lieutenant-general, in March 1942, McNair took command of army ground forces. This important position made him the supervisor for mobilizing and training the rapidly expanding US Army. This colossal task involved integrating Regular Army personnel with men from the National Guard and Army Reserve, and with new conscripts, to form a cohesive whole. At their peak, McNair controlled training facilities housing 1.5 million men. In addition, McNair supervised the conversion of the American infantry division from a square to a triangular formation featuring three, instead of four, major combat elements. His "special contribution was to enhance the mobility and flexibility of the new division." Although McNair's duties were administrative, he frequently visited troops at the front to see soldiers in action. During one such tour in Tunisia in 1943, he received a shrapnel wound.

McNair's mistaken analysis of the future of armored warfare condemned American tankers to use inferior weapons. Events would show that Sherman tanks (right, in the Ardennes in 1944) could fight the better German tanks only by overwhelming them with numbers. General Omar Bradley noted, "this willingness to expend Shermans offered little comfort to the crews who were forced to expend themselves as well." (US Army Military History Institute, Carlisle, PA)

Like many officers stuck in a rear area assignment, McNair agitated for a field command. In June 1944, he finally persuaded General Marshall to release him from army ground forces. Initially, McNair went to Britain to command the 1st Army Group, a nonexistent force used to dupe the Germans into thinking that a large army, with the capability of making a second invasion of the French coast, still remained in England. Then, McNair went to France to observe the aerial bombardment designed to open a gap for the breakout from Normandy. On July 23, 1944, misdirected bombs fell on McNair's observation post near St. Lo and killed him. He was the highest-ranking American officer ever killed in action.

Dubbed "the maker of armies" by his chief of staff, McNair was instrumental in converting the small regular army of the 1930s into the formidable force that helped defeat the Axis powers. More than any other individual, McNair was responsible for the strengths and weaknesses of the American Army, most notably its amazing flexibility and mobility at the price of inadequate combat power necessary for frontal assault.

Dwight David Eisenhower

Born in 1890 in Denison, Texas, Eisenhower spent his youth in Abilene, Kansas. "Ike" was one of seven sons in a poor, hard-working, religious family. Before he entered West Point, he spent a year supporting a brother in college. He graduated in 1915 and spent World War One on training duties. After completing various staff and school assignments, he became special assistant to Douglas MacArthur in Washington, DC, and the Philippines from 1933 to 1939. The outbreak of World War Two found him a brigadier-general, serving in the War Plans Division.

Then began a meteoric rise: major-general, April 1942; Commander US Forces Europe, June 1942; lieutenant-general, July 1942; general, February 1943; Supreme Commander Allied Expeditionary Force, December 1943; and general of the army, December 1944. In these

Eisenhower and Bradley (left rear) in Tunisia in 1943. (The George C. Marshall Research Library, Lexington, VA)

positions of increasing responsibility, Eisenhower matured as a leader, while supervising a fractious coalition. After the war, Eisenhower served as chief of staff until 1948 and then resigned to become President of Columbia University. He was recalled to active duty as Supreme Allied Commander in Europe in 1950. Two years later, he was elected to the first of his two terms as President of the United States. He died in 1969.

Because he lacked tactical and strategic brilliance, Eisenhower has often been dismissed by critics. In fact, he gave the Allied cause in Europe an indispensable mix of leadership and diplomacy so that divergent national interests and personalities could work toward the common goal of defeating Germany.

Walter Bedell Smith

Born in Indianapolis, Indiana in 1895, Walter Bedell Smith enlisted in the state's National Guard in 1910. He served in the Pershing Punitive Expedition to Mexico in 1916. A year later, he was fighting in France as a second lieutenant. While participating in an American offensive along the Marne in 1918, Smith received a shrapnel wound. Undaunted, he decided to make the military his career. Even though he never finished college, he proved a fine military administrator. The military took notice and sent him to both the Infantry School at Fort Benning and the Command and General Staff College at Fort Leavenworth. Smith earned a fine reputation and impressed General Marshall, who then brought him to Washington, DC, in 1939 to help organize the dramatically fast-growing American Army. Prior to this service, promotion had been slow. Marshall elevated him from major to brigadier-general within two years. Smith served as US Secretary of the Combined Chiefs of Staff until September 1942. Marshall wanted the no-nonsense Smith to serve with Eisenhower, and was pleased when the latter specifically asked for Smith to serve as his chief of staff at the time that Eisenhower began planning for the invasion of North Africa. Smith remained his chief of staff until the end of the European war.

In the words of one historian, "The two men formed an almost perfect relationship complementing each other's strengths." Eisenhower possessed a broad strategic vision. Smith, according to Eisenhower, was "a master of detail with the clear comprehension of main issues." Smith also buffered Eisenhower from distractions and personality clashes, so that his boss could concentrate on more weighty issues. He helped smooth the often tempestuous relations with the British. Aloof and quick tempered – a trait exacerbated by his chronic ulcers – Smith demonstrated surprising diplomatic skills.

After the war, President Truman, a fierce-tempered man himself, found a kindred spirit in this Midwestern leader. He chose Smith to serve as his ambassador to the Soviet Union from 1946 to 1949. In 1950, Smith became the Director of the Central Intelligence Agency. A year later, he received promotion to full general. It had been a long climb from an enlisted soldier in the Indiana National Guard. When Eisenhower was elected president, Smith served as Assistant Secretary of State to John Foster Dulles. It was a sign of Smith's diplomatic skills that he was one of very few to serve at a high level in both administrations.

Smith retired because of poor health in 1954 and died seven years later. Eisenhower himself provided the perfect eulogy, calling Smith, "one of the great staff chiefs of history, worthy to rank with Gneisenau."

Among George Marshall's talents for selecting officers was his understanding of personality. He knew the personable Eisenhower needed a tough chief of staff and so gave him General Bedell Smith. In this capacity, Smith served as a key adviser. He often handled delicate, important duties in Eisenhower's stead. Eisenhower called him "the general manager of the war." Smith signs the German surrender document in 1945. (The George C. Marshall Research Library, Lexington, VA)

John Clifford Hodges Lee

Born in Junction City, Kansas in 1887, John Lee graduated from West Point in 1909 with a commission in the prestigious Corps of Engineers. Before World War One, Lee earned a fine reputation for his engineering achievements while working on civil projects. He was smart and he knew it. Lee's triple initials and excessive self-regard gave rise among his army colleagues to the nickname, "Jesus Christ Himself." Lee served as an aide to General Leonard Wood from 1917 to 1918, and then as a staff officer with an infantry division in France. He saw action at St. Mihiel and Meuse-Argonne and won the Silver Star and Distinguished Service Medal. During the interwar years, Lee graduated from the Army War College and served as an instructor at the Army Industrial College.

Promoted to brigadier-general in 1940, ahead of Dwight D. Eisenhower, Lee commanded the 2d Infantry Division from November 1941 to May 1942. Promoted again, he went to England in May 1942. Lee failed to receive the field command he wanted and instead became

Eisenhower's logistics chief with the title Chief of Services for Supply in the European Theater of Operations. He held this position until the end of the war in Europe. In January 1944, Lee received the added duty of deputy theater commander of US forces.

As a logistics chief, Lee performed his work brilliantly. For example, in the fall of 1944 an artillery ammunition shortage hampered American operations. Unloading operations could not keep pace with demand. Autumn storms also disrupted port operation. Lee vigorously tackled these problems, set an urgent priority of unloading ammunition ships at Cherbourg, and established a 6,000-tons-daily overall goal for unloading. His effort paid off. From mid-October to mid-November daily discharges averaged 6,614 tons.

However, Lee's unlikable personality, and sometimes his judgment, caused problems. When the US armies massed on the continent, Eisenhower issued an order designed to limit civil-military conflict by keeping large numbers of American troops away from large cities. In early September 1944, Lee disregarded the order and moved his headquarters to Paris. He justified this move by arguing that Paris was the communications hub of France. However, by now he had earned a reputation as an "empire builder". Before Eisenhower could intervene, Lee's fast-moving billeting officers had requested Parisian accommodations for 8,000 officers and 21,000 enlisted men. Just as Eisenhower had anticipated, a great deal of negative publicity resulted from Lee's decision. Lee was briefly replaced but was soon reinstated. Still, criticism of his supply empire led to another major investigation in January 1945, but again the charges against him did not stick.

Eisenhower's chief logistics officer was the highly efficient John C. H. Lee. Lee was stern, arrogant, and so full of himself that soldiers referred to his initials and gave him the nickname "Jesus Christ Himself." Where American generals customarily wore their stars of rank on the front of their helmets, Lee wore a twin set: one in front and one on the back. Lee is shown here in Texas in 1942. (The George C. Marshall Research Library, Lexington, VA)

In December 1945, Lee transferred to the Mediterranean Theater of Operations, headquartered in Rome. A journalist wrote a highly critical, and not very accurate, series of articles claiming that Lee and his officers enjoyed the high life in Rome while the enlisted men suffered. Significantly, Eisenhower, who was now back in Washington, DC, did not defend Lee. The deeply religious Lee retired in 1947 and spent his remaining years working, largely outside of public view, with a lay Episcopalian group in Pennsylvania. He died in 1958.

During the time they worked together, Eisenhower publicly praised Lee as a "modern Cromwell" who had triumphed over an "appalling task." In private, Eisenhower did not like Lee. When Eisenhower rated his subordinates in February 1945, he placed Lee squarely in the middle of his senior generals with the comment, "a commander rather than a supply type; extremely loyal, energetic, tireless."

Omar Nelson Bradley

Born in 1893 in Clark, Missouri, the son of a schoolmaster, Omar Bradley, like Eisenhower, graduated from West Point in 1915. He saw no active service during World War One. Thereafter, he worked as a teacher of military science, including a four-year stint as an instructor at West Point from 1920 to 1924. The next year, he attended the Infantry School, at which time he attracted the favorable attention of George Marshall, and, in 1929, graduated first in a class of 88 from the Command and General Staff School. Until his promotion to brigadier-general in February 1941, Bradley held staff and teaching positions. The outbreak of World War Two found him commanding the Infantry School. Promoted to major-general in February 1942, Bradley thereafter served as commander of the 82d and 28th Divisions during the rapid expansion of the US Army. His skill as both teacher and organizer is shown by the fact that both divisions became outstanding fighting formations.

His rise to fame began when Marshall recommended that he join Eisenhower's staff to act as his "eyes and ears" during the North African campaign. When George Patton assumed corps command, Bradley acted as his deputy. Thereafter, Bradley took command of the 2d Corps during the mopping up operation in Tunisia and during the Sicilian campaign. He received promotion to lieutenant-general in June 1943. Eisenhower

Unlike most future senior commanders, Omar Bradley never led a unit in combat prior to World War Two. Inexperience and natural caution contributed to some poor decisions. For example, he later explained his decision to halt Patton's drive to close the Falaise Gap by saying that he wanted to avoid a head-on juncture of Canadian and American forces because such a juncture would have been "a dangerous and uncontrollable maneuver." The possibility of losses from friendly fire particularly worried Bradley. Bradley's cautious attitude does not seem justified by circumstances. Bradley (front center) is flanked on the left by Patton and Simpson and on the right by Courtney Hodges and Leonard Gerow, one of the premier US corps commanders. (National Archives)

respected Bradley's conduct and chose him to command the US 1st Army, the formation slotted to invade Normandy. As American forces in France grew, Bradley ascended to command the 12th Army Group. In this capacity, he commanded some 1.3 million men, more uniformed American troops than any other officer in history. In keeping with his reputation for caring for his soldiers, after the war, Bradley directed the Veterans Administration until 1947. He then became chief of staff for the army, and chairman of the Joint Chiefs of Staff from 1949 to 1953. In this capacity, he directed the grand strategy of the Korean War. He became general of the army in 1950. He died in 1981.

Bradley (center) meets with corps commander Troy Middleton (left) and Eisenhower (right) in Wiltz, November 1944. None of these officers suspected that Wiltz would fall to the surprise German offensive the next month. (US Army Military History Institute, Carlisle, PA)

Bradley had to cope with logistical and manpower problems on an enormous scale as well as handle frequent disagreements with the detested Montgomery. It is difficult to assess Bradley as a military strategist. As a commander, he was cool, quiet, cautious, and orthodox in his approach to war, while always showing a fierce dedication to the well-being and reputation of the American Army. He was also involved in controversial decisions. These included: the August 1944 decisionto halt Patton's 15th Corps at Argentan, which permitted the Germans to escape from certain destruction in the Falaise pocket; his advocacy of the broad front approach to Germany; and his quarrel with Montgomery over the response to the German offensive in the Ardennes and the subsequent handling of the Allied counter-offensive. The conventional evaluation, not shared by this author, ranks Bradley as "one of the most talented commanders in American military history."

George Smith Patton Jr

Born in 1885 in San Gabriel, California, George Patton came from a long line of soldiers. His grandfather and six great-uncles had been Confederate officers. Patton attended the Virginia Military Institute for a year before going on to graduate from West Point in 1909. He accompanied the 1916 Pershing Expedition and killed two of Pancho Villa's men in a gunfight. He returned to

Patton and Russian General Zhukov. Note the contrast in chest medals. Patton's self-vision as a great captain who should die from the "last bullet of the last war" did not occur. Instead, he died in his sleep in December 1945. (National Archives)

OPPOSITE BELOW **The "most colorful and controversial American general in the European Theater." Patton is riding a captured horse originally intended as a gift from Hitler to the Japanese Emperor Hirohito. Patton was an outstanding rider and athlete, having been placed fifth in the modern pentathlon at the 1912 Olympics. (National Archives)**

BELOW **"In an unequaled dash across France... the 3d Army drove back the German defenders 600 miles in thirty days." George Patton is shown with French civilians. (National Archives)**

headquarters with their bodies strapped to the hood of an automobile, to claim flamboyantly that he had led the "first motorized attack in history." Pershing took Patton to France in 1917, where Patton organized the newly established US Army's Tank Corps. Patton led his tank unit into combat, exhibited fearless front-line leadership, was wounded, and earned the Distinguished Service Cross for valor. During the interwar years, Patton continued his martial studies and served in a variety of command and staff positions. When George Marshall created the US Armored Force in July 1940, he assigned Patton brigade command in the new 2d Armored Division. Elevated to divisional command at the rank of major-general, Patton's "Hell on Wheels" division excelled during large-scale maneuvers in the summer of 1941.

After Pearl Harbor, Patton assumed command of the 1st Armored Corps. His knowledge of amphibious warfare led to his appointment to the planning staff for Operation Torch. Subsequently, Patton commanded the Western Task Force in the assault into Morocco on November 8, 1942. In March 1943, Eisenhower reassigned Patton to command of the demoralized 2d Corps, the force that had fought at Kasserine Pass. Patton characteristically whipped this force into fighting shape and led it successfully in the assault into Tunisia. Promoted to lieutenant-general in April 1943, Patton took the 7th Army into Sicily. His aggressive and often brilliant leadership placed him at the forefront of American combat leaders. However, the infamous incident when he slapped two soldiers suffering from combat fatigue, while touring a hospital almost ended his career. Only his long-standing friendship with Eisenhower saved him.

Patton did not return to active duty until August 1, 1944 when the 3d Army was activated in France. He led this force in a brilliant drive to the German border. He again distinguished himself in December 1944 at the Battle of the Bulge. In an impressive feat of logistical management and planning, Patton turned his army 90 degrees and drove nearly 100 miles in deepest winter to attack the German left flank and relieve Bastogne. In late January, Patton's army resumed the drive to the east, crossed the Rhine on March 22, drove through the heart of Germany at the rate of 30 miles a day, and reached the outskirts of Prague by the war's end.

Patton's inclination to use former Nazis as civil administrators led to his relief. He died on December 21, 1945 from complications resulting from an automobile accident. Throughout his career, Patton displayed a willingness to exceed orders while pursuing his offensive vision. An assessment of Patton is perhaps best left to his enemies: of all Allied ground commanders in World War Two, the bold and aggressive George Patton was the leader whom the Germans most feared.

Mark Wayne Clark

The son of a military officer, Mark Clark was born in Madison Barracks, New York, in 1896. Entering West Point in 1913, he soon made many friends among officers who were to assume high responsibility during World War Two. Clark graduated in 1917 with an infantry commission and went to France. Here, he received a wound that rendered him officially unfit for combat. He spent the remainder of the war dealing with the frustration of a rear area assignment. A brigadier-general in August 1941, Clark began a rapid ascent that made him numerous enemies. In

BELOW **Mark Clark's (left) first important wartime service was a secret diplomatic mission to Algeria to negotiate with French leaders in preparation for the Allied invasion of North Africa. He made the controversial decision to work with Admiral Jean Darlan. Among many, Charles de Gaulle (center) did not like it. (National Archives)**

BELOW RIGHT **Mark Clark's fixation on symbolic objectives, such as capturing Rome, led many to conclude "that he unnecessarily risked soldiers' lives in an erratic campaign that was waged primarily to secure his selfish objectives." Clark with Admiral Alan Kirk. (National Archives)**

March 1942, he was appointed acting chief of staff of US Army ground forces. The next month saw him promoted to major-general. He became nominal commander of all Europe-based US ground forces in July.

After conducting a secret diplomatic mission to Algeria, Clark was promoted to lieutenant-general in November 1942. Clark pressed General Eisenhower for a field command and in January 1943, Clark assumed command of the US 5th Army. He held this position throughout the Italian campaign. Clark's tenure as army commander was plagued by criticism of his selfish behavior. In part, this criticism came from jealous peers who believed that Clark had been promoted too fast. Numerous controversies ensued, including questions about the disastrous assault across the Rapido River and the stalemate at Anzio and Cassino. Clark was pressured to accept command of the 7th Army and direct the invasion of southern France. He utilized all of his connections to remain with the 5th Army so that he could seize Rome. In the event, he disobeyed General Harold Alexander's orders, in a misguided effort to enter Rome ahead of the British. The 5th Army finally entered Rome on June 5, 1944. In December 1944, Clark became commander of the 15th Army Group, a formation operating in northern Italy, composed of soldiers from many countries, including Americans, British, Poles, Indians, and Brazilians. Following Clark's promotion to full general in March 1945, this army group swept across the Po Valley in April. Clark personally accepted the surrender of German forces in Italy.

After the war, Clark served as commander of occupied Austria, eliminating Nazi influences while working successfully to keep Austria outside of the Soviet orbit. Thereafter, Clark held a variety of senior posts including, most importantly, two positions during the Korean War: Commander-in-Chief of the UN Command and then US Commander-in-Chief in the Far East. He signed the armistice at Panmunjon in July 1953 and retired the following October. From 1954 to 1960, he was president of The Citadel, a prestigious South Carolina military academy, and spent his final years as Chairman of the American Battle Monuments Commission. Clark died in 1984.

Clark was among the most controversial of senior American generals. Neither Eisenhower nor Patton liked or respected him since both shared the view that his ambition overcame his judgment. Among Clark's supporters was Winston Churchill, who called him the "American Eagle."

Courtney Hicks Hodges

Born in Perry, Georgia in 1887, Courtney Hodges attended West Point for two years before having to withdraw because he could not handle the mathematics. He then enlisted as a private and earned his second-lieutenant's commission in 1909, only

During his tenure as chief of infantry, Courtney Hodges promoted the adoption of the hand-held anti-tank weapon, the bazooka, the M-1 carbine, and the use of airborne troops. (National Archives)

A careful tactician, Hodges responded well to the surprise German offensive through the Ardennes. On December 17, 1944 he called Bradley to request the 101st and 82d Airborne Divisions. Bradley responded plaintively saying that they were Eisenhower's only reserves. Hodges replied, "I've got to have them." The subsequent release of these divisions saved the American position in the Ardennes. On January 19, 1945 Bradley adds a cluster to Hodges' Distinguished Service Medal in honor of Hodges' leadership in the Ardennes. (US Army Military History Institute, Carlisle, PA)

a year after his nominal West Point class graduated. Hodges served with the Pershing Punitive Expedition to Mexico and with the infantry in France in World War One. He proved himself to be a good combat soldier, received promotion to lieutenant-colonel, and earned a Distinguished Service Cross. Between the wars, Hodges was an instructor at West Point and was General Omar Bradley's immediate predecessor as the commandant of the Infantry School at Fort Benning. In May 1941, he was promoted to major-general and became chief of infantry.

During the war's first years, he held corps command and headed the army ground forces school system. Promoted to lieutenant-general in February 1943, Hodges took command of the US 3d Army in Britain. The following January, he became Bradley's deputy. When Bradley ascended to army group commander, Hodges replaced him as commander of the 1st Army. Bradley bequeathed Hodges, who was himself an irascible man, talented but prickly staff. Bradley could control them but Hodges could not. First Army staff caused repeated problems for the remainder of the war. Hodges led his army through northern France to Belgium, where they ground to a halt before the Siegfried Line. The bloody battle for Aachen and the Roer River dams ensued, followed by the Battle of the Bulge. Like all senior US leaders, from Eisenhower down, Hodges was surprised by the German offensive through the Ardennes. However, he responded well to the crisis and, on the offensive's second day, December 17, made the key request for the two airborne divisions that plugged the holes in his line and saved the key crossroads town of Bastogne. Thereafter, his army advanced over the Remagen Bridge into Germany to meet Soviet forces on the Elbe River in March 1945. Through it all, Hodges showed little patience for faltering subordinates and even relieved a corps commander. After being promoted to full general, Hodges retired in 1949 and died in 1966.

Bradley considered Hodges to be a calm and careful infantry tactician. Others disagreed, believing Hodges was too quick to yield to his over-bearing staff and too cautious. One historian has fairly assessed Hodges as "a competent operational commander who tended to be methodical."

Jacob Loucks Devers

Born in York, Pennsylvania in 1887, Jacob Devers was an outstanding athlete during his days at West Point. He graduated in 1909 with an artillery commission. Devers spent World War One at the School of Fire at Fort Sill. He believed that, because he did not serve in combat in France, his career was ruined. During the interwar years, Devers completed the usual school assignments and held a series of staff and training positions.

General Marshall noted Devers' abilities and gave him three key assignments, beginning in June 1939 when he made Devers chief of staff of the Panama Canal Department. In this capacity, Devers jumped ahead of 474 other colonels to receive promotion to brigadier-general. Devers returned to Washington, DC, in July 1940 as a senior army member of the board that chose the bases in the Destroyers for Bases deal with Great Britain. Next, Marshall gave Devers a coveted line assignment as commander of the 9th Infantry Division at Fort Bragg. Devers supervised a 300 percent expansion of Fort Bragg and was promoted to major-general. In July 1941, Marshall appointed Devers chief of Armored Force. Devers had spent over two decades in the artillery. However, he quickly adjusted to a new style of mobile warfare. He worked to coordinate all arms mobile warfare, with particular emphasis on close cooperation between ground and air units. He notably went against standard doctrine, as promoted by General Lesley McNair, by advocating the development of heavier tanks with greater firepower and armor.

Holding the rank of lieutenant-general, Devers was named overall commander of the European Theater of Operations in May 1943. He spent the remainder of the year in England, supervising the training and planning for the invasion of France. He hoped to lead this great effort personally but was passed over in favor of Eisenhower. At the end of 1943, Devers went to the Mediterranean Theater as Deputy Supreme Allied Commander. He finally got his first combat command in September 1944, when he became commander of the 6th Army Group. This was the force that had invaded southern France. The force comprised the US 7th Army and the French 1st Army. Devers displayed good management ability by uniquely organizing an efficient, lean, and mobile headquarters that avoided duplication of function with subordinate headquarters.

George Marshall (left) identified Jacob Devers (right) as a talented leader and handed him key assignments beginning in 1939. (National Archives)

Devers in Italy with a Polish machine gunner. (National Archives)

Although Devers was the equal in rank of Montgomery and Bradley, he was not one of Eisenhower's trusted confidants. His army group operated on the right of the Allied line facing the German border, a decidedly secondary front. Many of Devers' most difficult challenges came from his contact with his prickly French subordinate, General Jean de Lattre de Tassigny, and the prideful General Charles de Gaulle. Devers' most significant combat command decisions involved opposing the German offensive, Operation Nordwind, in December 1944 and early January 1945.

Devers received a fourth star, the rank of full general, in March 1945. He ably conducted his army's offensive over the Rhine on March 26, 1945. The advance continued across southern Germany and into Austria where, on May 6, Devers accepted the surrender of all German forces in the region.

After the war, Devers served for four years as commander of US Army ground forces. He retired in 1949 and died in 1979. During the war years, the affable Devers displayed a common sense approach to problem solving. He also displayed good management and notable diplomatic skills when dealing with the French. He never fully gained Eisenhower's trust, perhaps because of the issue of Eisenhower superceding Devers in England. In addition, Devers operated on a secondary front and, consequently, never received the same acclaim as more prominent senior leaders.

Alexander McCarrell Patch

Alexander "Sandy" Patch was born in Fort Huachuca, Arizona in 1889. He graduated from West Point with an infantry commission in 1913. After service on the Mexican border in 1916, Patch commanded a machine gun battalion in France during World War One. During the interwar years, Patch worked as an instructor of military science and graduated from both the Command and General Staff College and the Army War College. He received promotion to brigadier-general in December 1940 and, subsequently, performed training duty at Fort Bragg. He was promoted to major-general in March 1942, and went to the Pacific, where he organized and trained the Americal Division. After the Marines had won the defensive battle on Guadalcanal, Patch assumed command on the island on December 9, 1942. After he secured the island, poor health forced Patch to return to the States, where he commanded the 4th Corps and the Desert Training Center.

Promoted to lieutenant-general in August 1944, Patch took command of the 7th Army for the invasion of southern France. He led the army up the Rhone Valley to link up with Eisenhower's main body along the German border. His army helped form the southern pincer in the colossal envelopment of German forces during the final push across the Rhine. After the defeat of Germany, Patch received command of the 4th Army in the Pacific as it prepared for the invasion of Japan. He died in November 1945 and received a posthumous promotion to full general in 1954.

Because his army entered France via "the back door" and thereafter assumed a position on a secondary front, Patch never received the attention and acclaim of some other senior American commanders.

Devers' greatest challenge came during the German offensive, Operation Nordwind. The French wanted to hold the line and, in particular, defend Strasbourg. Eisenhower wanted Devers to yield ground so that American forces could mass against the Germans in the Ardennes. This led to confusion and hesitation and prompted Eisenhower to instruct Bedell Smith, "Call up Devers and tell him he is not doing what he was told to do." Devers in the winter snows in France. (National Archives)

RIGHT Unlike more self-promoting generals, Patch was easy-going by nature. When Eisenhower once asked if he minded that Patton's army wanted to advance across Patch's 7th Army boundary, Patch replied that he did not object, saying, "We are all the same army." (National Archives)

Alexander Patch (right, next to George Marshall) gained prominence when he relieved the Marines on Guadalcanal. He devised a pincer operation to capture the Japanese forces but failed to appreciate that he was facing a rear guard intent on covering the Japanese evacuation of the island. Consequently, the pincers closed on empty ground. Still, Patch proudly reported to Admiral Halsey on February 9, 1943, "Tokyo Express no longer has terminus on Guadalcanal." (National Archives)

William Hood Simpson

Born in Weatherford, Texas in 1888, William "Texas Bill" Simpson graduated from West Point in 1909. For the next three years, he served in the Philippines. In 1916, he was with the Pershing Punitive Expedition to Mexico and then was a staff officer with an infantry division in France. During the interwar years, Simpson completed the necessary school assignments and, from 1936 until 1940, was an instructor at the Army War College. America's entrance into the war found Simpson in command of the 30th and 35th Infantry Divisions. Following a stateside corps and army command, Simpson finally entered an active theater when he went to England in May 1944. His assignment was to organize the formations that became the 9th Army.

The 9th Army's 8th Corps, under the command of Troy Middleton, entered combat in Brittany in September 1944. Thereafter, the army advanced toward the German border. Eisenhower wanted to make the main effort north of the Ardennes, with the 1st Army providing the main thrust. Accordingly, he inserted Simpson's army between the British and the American 1st Army. Simpson's assignment was to reach the Rhine River and then turn northward to assist the British. In its first major campaign in November and early December 1944, the 9th Army failed to achieve a breakthrough. However, it cleared the west bank of the Roer River throughout its sector in a professional

manner. It emulated its leader by operating with quiet efficiency and made no major mistakes. Simpson also displayed an unusual ability to cooperate with the antagonistic British Field Marshal Montgomery. This trust influenced the planning behind Operation Grenade, the assault crossing of the Rhine. Simpson's army received major reinforcements, to bring its manpower total to over 300,000 for this operation. It also enjoyed the largest concentration of guns an American army had yet gathered for an offensive. The 9th Army advanced farther into Germany than any American army, before halting to meet the Soviets at the Elbe River.

Simpson retired from the army in 1955 and died in 1980. Simpson's extensive staff and academic experience and his low-key personality influenced his command style. He built a solid staff team, had his chief of staff execute his ideas, and relied upon his subordinates to accomplish their missions without meddling. He was a competent, but not brilliant, leader. Bradley praised Simpson, saying that he had the easiest army headquarters to work with. Even higher praise came from Eisenhower: Simpson "was the type of leader American soldiers deserve."

Because of the performance of William Simpson's 9th Army, which contrasted with Patton's flamboyant but erratic 3d Army and Hodges' prima-donna-like 1st Army, General Bradley concluded that he could rely upon Simpson to accomplish missions in a business-like manner. Bradley pins a bronze star on Simpson. (National Archives)

Lucian King Truscott Jr

Born in Chatfield, Texas in 1895, Lucian Truscott entered the army without the benefit of any formal military education. He was teaching school when America entered World War One. He enlisted in the army and was selected for officer training. He served as a cavalry lieutenant on the Mexican border during the war. His background as a teacher, and his cavalry service, led to his assignment as instructor at the Cavalry School from 1927 to 1931. He was a polo-playing friend of George Patton and played on the national polo team in 1934. Between the wars, Truscott stood out enough to warrant his attendance at the Command and General Staff College. He was an instructor at this school when World War Two began. After a brief stint as executive officer in an armored battalion, Truscott served as a general staff officer until May 1942.

General Marshall arranged for an American section to be attached to the vaunted British commando forces led by Admiral Louis Mountbatten. Promoted to brigadier-general, Truscott received an assignment as American liaison officer to the British Combined Operations forces. His special responsibility was to keep abreast of British amphibious equipment and methods.

Truscott proposed that the American equivalent of the British commandos be called "Rangers." The name stuck and Truscott assumed responsibility for organizing and training the 1st Ranger Battalion. When 50 American Rangers took part in the raid on Dieppe, Truscott went along. In November 1942, Truscott led a special task force in the capture of a port in French Morocco. This was a particularly difficult operation because his force had to land from the sea, cross

the beach, and then re-embark in boats to cross another waterway.

Promoted to major-general, Truscott was field deputy to General Eisenhower during the Tunisian campaign in the winter of 1942–43. In March 1943, Truscott assumed command of the 3d Infantry Division. He led this division during the invasion of Sicily. Meticulous staff planning characterized the division's amphibious landing. The division next landed at Salerno after the beaches were secured and, subsequently, participated in the Anzio landings.

When Lieutenant-General John Lucas faltered at Anzio, Truscott took his place as commander of the 6th Corps on February 22, 1944. Truscott injected new vigor into the corps and was a pivotal figure in preventing an Allied debacle at Anzio. He led the corps in the May 1944 breakout from the Anzio beachhead. By the time his corps entered Rome on June 4, Truscott's performance had earned sufficient favorable attention from both Eisenhower and General Omar Bradley that

At the time when Eisenhower inspected General Lucian Truscott's 3d Infantry Division in Tunisia, one of Eisenhower's aides wrote in his diary that Eisenhower "thinks highly of Truscott." Truscott (right, next to Mark Clark) in Italy in 1944. (The George C. Marshall Research Library, Lexington, VA)

Truscott typically wore unorthodox dress: shiny enameled helmet, weather stained jacket with a white silk scarf, and faded dress cavalry breeches (shown here) that he considered "lucky." Truscott inspects the newly arrived all black 92d Infantry Division in Italy. (The George C. Marshall Research Library, Lexington, VA)

leaders saw him as a potential army commander. The 6th Corps landed in southern France on August 15, 1944 as the major American component of the Anvil-Dragoon landings. It advanced up the Rhone Valley toward the Belfort Gap and then merged with the main front along the German border.

Truscott's ability propelled him to army command in December 1944 when he returned to Italy to take over command of the 5th Army from General Mark Clark. Although Italy was very much a "side show" at this time, Truscott directed the army in the drive across the Po Valley. He had the satisfaction of capturing Bologna on April 21, 1945. After the inactivation of the 5th Army, Truscott succeeded General Patton as commander of the 3d Army on garrison duty in Bavaria. He received promotion to full general in 1954, when he was on the retired list, and died in 1965.

Truscott combined a school teacher's meticulous approach to work with the dash of a cavalryman. He adapted very well to the special challenges of amphibious warfare. Because he served in Italy and southern France, he did not have as much opportunity to distinguish himself as did commanders on the main fronts.

Douglas MacArthur

The son of a distinguished American Civil War general, Douglas MacArthur was born in 1880 at an army post near Little Rock, Arkansas. MacArthur attended West Point and graduated first in his class in 1903. He served with distinction in World War One, received several decorations for bravery, and ended the war as the youngest American divisional commander. The American Secretary of War, and many reporters, described him as the army's best front-line general. This was music to MacArthur's ears because throughout his career he exhibited an unstinting quest for publicity.

MacArthur returned from Europe to receive a plum assignment, superintendent of West Point. In 1930, he served as army chief of staff. Two years later, he personally supervised the army's brutal eviction of World War One veterans, the so-called bonus army, from Washington, DC. After retiring as chief of staff, MacArthur served for three frustrating years as Field Marshal for the Army of the Philippine Commonwealth. During this time, he became close friends with the Philippine President, Manuel Quezon. In the summer of 1941, President Roosevelt called the Army of the Philippine Commonwealth into the service of the United States. To command the new organization, "US Army Forces, Far East," Roosevelt recalled MacArthur to active service.

At this time, American strategy recognized that the Philippines could not be held against a Japanese attack. The best that could be hoped was for the American and Philippine forces to fight a delaying action. MacArthur argued persuasively that the Philippines could be successfully

General Douglas MacArthur was, arguably, the most controversial senior American leader. His World War Two service began in the Philippines. Rather than concede everything except the defense of Manila Bay, as called for in all prior planning, MacArthur wanted to meet the invaders on the beaches; there was to be "no withdrawal from beach positions. The beaches were to be held at all costs." This effort failed dismally. (National Archives)

defended. In the event, MacArthur's plan was hopelessly over-optimistic. Although some Filipino units fought splendidly, the balance were untrained and poorly equipped. They proved no match for the Japanese veterans. Two days after the main Japanese landings on Luzon, MacArthur ordered a general retreat to Bataan. However, because of MacArthur's insistence upon a forward defense, nothing had been done to prepare for this move.

A summary of MacArthur's performance in the Philippines can only be damning. He had allowed his air force to be crippled on the ground during the war's first day. His grandiose plan to defend everything had led to confusion and near disaster. It also caused a terrible supply shortage for the Bataan defenders. During the fighting on Bataan, MacArthur visited his front-line troops only once, thereby earning the nickname "Dugout Doug." While safely ensconced on Corregidor, he issued reports to the American people. A total of 109 of 142 communiqués mentioned only one individual: MacArthur. Yet the American people were so desperate for a hero at this black hour that Roosevelt and Marshall awarded him the Congressional Medal of Honor and made sure that he was evacuated to Australia.

In violation of the principle of unity of command, the Pacific was divided into two theaters and MacArthur was appointed Commander-in-Chief of the Southwest Pacific area. This area embraced Australia, the Philippines, the Solomons, New Guinea, the Bismark Archipelago, Borneo, and all of the Dutch East Indies except Sumatra. MacArthur staffed his command with trusted officers, the so-called "Bataan Gang." Too often, many of these officers acted like sycophants, supporting MacArthur's ambition, to the detriment of the war effort.

MacArthur's vision remained firmly fixated on the Philippines. On September 15, 1944 he landed a mere two hours after the first wave invaded Morotai. Gazing across the 300 miles that separated him from the Philippines he said, "They are waiting for me there. It has been a long time." The famous, carefully staged return of Douglas MacArthur to the Philippines in October 1944. (National Archives)

MacArthur's first assignment was to secure Australia from Japanese invasion. He understood that Port Moresby, on the southern coast of Papua New Guinea, was a key forward position. Because he had been told that the ground was impassable, the Japanese advance over the Owen Stanley Mountains against Port Moresby surprised and frightened MacArthur. "Hap" Arnold saw him at this time and wrote, "His hands twitch and tremble – shell shocked." MacArthur rallied to supervise the Australian and American counter-offensive in New Guinea, which drove the Japanese back to Buna and Gona. Here, terrible terrain and tenacious defense shattered all attacks. MacArthur remained back at his headquarters in Australia. He had no idea about the real situation at the front and, instead, blamed a lack of fighting spirit for the setbacks. His insistence on repeated frontal attacks by infantry who lacked heavy weapons and tanks caused heavy Allied losses. The Buna campaign involved six months of bitter fighting and cost some 8,500 casualties, including 3,000 dead.

MacArthur recognized some of the mistakes. In particular, he accepted General Kenney's assertion that air superiority was the necessary prerequisite to all other operations. MacArthur also adopted a "leapfrog strategy," whereby his forces would bypass Japanese strongholds. During operations against Lae and Salamaua, MacArthur overcame a lack of naval resources and terrible terrain with brilliant innovation involving small-scale amphibious operations and the use of airborne forces. His strategy confused the Japanese and kept them off balance. Nevertheless, MacArthur correctly sensed that Nimitz's campaign through the central Pacific was proceeding faster and better. His own goal was Rabaul, yet planners were already contemplating bypassing this Japanese fortress. With characteristic myopia, MacArthur argued that he had to have Rabaul to secure his flank and to use as a base. Fortunately, wiser heads prevailed. As the chief US naval historian wrote, "Tarawa, Iwo Jima, and Okinawa would have faded to pale pink in comparison with the blood which would have flowed if the Allies had attempted an assault on fortress Rabaul." To jump-start his own campaign, MacArthur took a gamble by attacking the Admiralties. Although the gamble succeeded, historians have criticized it as reckless.

MacArthur managed to win the strategic debate about whether to attack the Philippines or Formosa. Although Marshall and King favored Formosa, MacArthur, apparently, convinced Roosevelt that the Philippines should be the next objective. Logistical considerations also favored the Philippines. When Admiral Halsey's carrier strikes revealed the weakness of Japanese air power in the Philippines, the Joint Chiefs set an October date for the invasion of Leyte. At first, the invasion of Leyte went very well but Japanese resistance stiffened and the ground advance became bogged down.

On August 14, 1945, MacArthur was named Supreme Commander of the Allied Powers, thus

MacArthur observes the signing of the Japanese surrender in Tokyo Bay. MacArthur served as military governor of Japan. He handled this job brilliantly and introduced numerous reforms. It proved the high point of his career. (US Naval Historical Center)

making him responsible for accepting the Japanese surrender in Tokyo. Thereafter, he was in charge of Japan's demilitarization and economic rebuilding. During the Korean War, MacArthur was named Supreme Commander. His bold amphibious invasion at Inchon permitted the US forces to drive the North Koreans out of South Korea. Thereafter, he made a colossal strategic error by ignoring the possibility of Chinese intervention. MacArthur's noisy criticism of US policy and of President Truman caused him to be removed in April 1951. Shortly before his death in 1964, MacArthur spoke to the cadets at West Point. His eloquent words described the academy's core values: "Duty, Honor, Country."

In summary, MacArthur was an inspiring, vainglorious leader whose self-confidence and ambition interfered with sound military judgment. However, to his credit, he adapted to military change, utilized air power well, and mastered amphibious operations.

Richard Kerens Sutherland

Born in 1893 in Hancock, Maryland, Richard Sutherland graduated from Yale in 1916 and was commissioned in the infantry. He served with the 2d Division in France during World War One. Between the wars, Sutherland taught military science and attended the US Army's top command schools as well as France's Ecole Supérieure de Guerre. July 1941 saw both promotion to brigadier-general and assignment as Douglas MacArthur's chief of staff. Sutherland brought a formidable intellect to the challenge of serving on MacArthur's staff. He conceived that MacArthur required someone to be the "tough guy," a "hard-driving disciplinarian" who would not be concerned about personal popularity. Sutherland undertook this task himself. He rigorously ran staff meetings, defining problems and assigning teams to solve them. However, his own arrogance and temper often got in the way. Like his chief, Sutherland enjoyed the prerogatives of command. For example, the train carrying the headquarters' staff to their new base in Australia included a flatcar loaded with MacArthur's gleaming limousine as well as Sutherland's only slightly more modest Cadillac.

Sutherland began the war on a controversial note. He refused to allow MacArthur's air commander, General Lewis Brereton, to meet with MacArthur to discuss an immediate air attack against Japanese airfields in Formosa. Indecision and hesitation led to the destruction of Brereton's command. In the days following the outbreak of war, Sutherland acted as MacArthur's deputy commander. He made more tactical decisions than MacArthur and had a better grasp of what was really taking place on the ground. Sutherland organized the escape of the Philippine President, Manuel Quezon, and later persuaded MacArthur to comply with President Roosevelt's order to depart the Philippines. He then selected the key personnel, including himself, who accompanied the general.

General Richard Sutherland at MacArthur's headquarters in the Corregidor tunnel. Sutherland interfered with General Brereton's plan for a pre-emptive strike on Japanese airbases and shared responsibility for the disastrous loss of most of Brereton's modern planes, which were destroyed on the ground. (National Archives)

In Australia, Sutherland rebuilt MacArthur's staff and exercised imperious control over them. In late 1942, MacArthur sent Sutherland to investigate why the Allied offensive against Buna and Gona was stalled. Sutherland failed to appreciate that terrible terrain and lack of heavy weapons and tanks accounted for the absence of progress. Instead, he unjustly blamed an American divisional commander, whom MacArthur then removed from command. Thereafter, Sutherland's job changed from grand tactical concerns to strategic planning and liaison with the Joint Chiefs of Staff. Because Sutherland lacked tact, and disliked the navy, this liaison role proved troublesome.

In March 1943, MacArthur sent Sutherland to Washington, DC, to argue his position regarding an offensive against Rabaul. Sutherland claimed that the effort required five more divisions and 1,800 planes. This claim shocked American planners. Sutherland's abrasive personality made planning sessions tense.

Back in Australia, Sutherland continued to behave imperiously. He overrode official resistance and written regulations by falsely insisting that he had MacArthur's approval to promote his Australian mistress into the Women's Auxiliary Air Corps. In addition, because he believed that he uniquely understood MacArthur's plans, he began to act on his own initiative. For example, during the planning for the invasion of the Philippines, Sutherland made important decisions in MacArthur's name, at a critical time when MacArthur was absent aboard a cruiser that was observing radio silence. Sutherland did this to promote MacArthur's strategy but he also, knowingly, minimized the amount of likely Japanese resistance even though his intelligence officers had provided a more accurate assessment. Quite simply, Sutherland believed that he knew better than everyone else.

Sutherland finally fell badly afoul of his chief when he disobeyed MacArthur's orders twice, by bringing his mistress to the Philippines, and was caught both times. A towering argument ensued, with MacArthur placing his chief of staff under arrest. Yet, by the next day, Sutherland was back at work. Still, this incident probably kept Sutherland from receiving a coveted army command. Sutherland became disillusioned with his boss and, subsequently, performed his duties poorly. Everyone except MacArthur thought that he should be relieved. Finally, by the late summer of 1945, MacArthur allowed Sutherland to return home on leave. A week later, Japan surrendered and MacArthur quickly recalled him to restore order to his staff, who were suddenly overwhelmed by new and unfamiliar duties. Sutherland performed this task admirably. Sutherland remained in Japan with MacArthur for three months and then departed for good.

His hopes for army command were never achieved and Sutherland left the army a bitter man. He had won no glory and made no friends. Yet, he had started the war as a lieutenant-colonel and ended it a lieutenant-general. Throughout this time, he was the driving force in MacArthur's staff and widely regarded as the "power behind the throne." Sutherland retired from the army in 1946 and died in 1966.

Joseph Warren Stilwell

Born in 1883 in Palatka, Florida, Joseph Stilwell received a commission in the infantry from West Point in 1904. Following two tours of duty in the Philippines, he served with the American Expeditionary Force in France as deputy chief of staff for intelligence. Stilwell studied Chinese in Peking from 1920 to 1923. Three years later, he graduated from the Command and General Staff School at Fort Leavenworth. Between 1926 and 1929, Stilwell served with American forces stationed in China. His next assignment, as instructor at the Infantry School, brought him into contact with George Marshall, who was the head of the school. Stilwell returned to China in 1935 for a four-year assignment as military attaché.

Stilwell in China with Nationalist leader Chiang Kai-shek and the influential Madame Chiang Kai-shek. Stilwell brought to his difficult assignment important skills and significant liabilities. He had long experience in China and spoke the language fluently. He thoroughly understood convoluted Chinese politics. He genuinely liked and respected Chinese soldiers and appreciated their strengths and weaknesses. However, he was short tempered, impatient, and a poor administrator. Logistics, staff work, and planning did not interest him. He loathed all paper work. Stilwell also demanded total loyalty from his staff, which encouraged sycophancy rather than sharp analysis and criticism. He designed a mock award, the "Order of the Rat," to be hung from a double cross for officers who requested transfer, or, in Stilwell's words, "who ran out on us."(The George C. Marshall Research Library, Lexington, VA)

The attack on Pearl Harbor found Stilwell a major-general in command of the 2d Corps.

General Marshall and the US Secretary of State sought a senior officer to represent the United States in the China Theater. They selected Stilwell. Stilwell did not want to go to China, particularly because Marshall had slated him for an important command in Europe. However, on March 10, 1942, he agreed to "go where I'm sent." Holding the rank of lieutenant-general, Stilwell was in charge of US Army forces in China, Burma, and India and supervised American assistance to the Chinese war effort.

By the time Stilwell arrived in China, the Japanese had already seized Rangoon and severed the Burma Road. The Nationalist Chinese leader, Chiang Kai-shek, made Stilwell his chief of staff and sent him to Burma. The subsequent effort to defend Burma failed disastrously. Stilwell and his staff had to march 140 miles through mountain and jungle to escape to India. Stilwell candidly told reporters, "I claim we got a hell of a beating." He set out to determine why and to fix the problems.

The defeat in Burma reaffirmed Stilwell's belief that the Chinese Army needed massive reform and reorganization. The Japanese conquest of Burma had severed the last overland supply route to China. Consequently, Stilwell's strategy for the next 18 months centered on reopening China's lines of communication, including a counter-offensive into Burma as soon as possible. Until that occurred, the long and difficult flight over the Himalayas, "flying the Hump," was the only avenue for supplies to reach China. The daunting logistics of moving

Because of the toughness of his training programs at Fort Bragg, General Joseph Stilwell earned the nickname "Vinegar Joe." He demonstrated this toughness while leading the 140-mile trek from Burma to safety in India in 1942. (The George C. Marshall Research Library, Lexington, VA)

American lend-lease supplies from India to China caused Stilwell to devise an innovative scheme as a stopgap measure. Figuring that it was easier to move the men to the supplies rather than the supplies to the men, he had the planes carrying supplies to China make the return trip loaded with Chinese recruits. In this way, ill-fed, sick, and nearly naked Chinese soldiers came to India, where "they were fed for the first time with as much food and meat as they could stuff into their hungry bodies. They practiced on ranges with live shells and real bullets... hospitals doctored them." Under Stilwell's program, by 1944, four very effective Chinese divisions had been created and trained in India. Stilwell planned to use these forces to recapture Burma. In addition, American engineer teams, directed by Stilwell's chief engineer, General Lewis Pick, labored in the rear of advancing Chinese forces to build the Ledo Road. When completed, "Pick's Pike" would connect with the Burma Road and provide a land supply route to China.

In April 1943, Stilwell and the American air commander in China, General Claire Chennault, went to Washington, DC, to participate in strategic planning. Stilwell did not like Roosevelt. He regarded the president as a meddling amateur, and was sullen and uncommunicative. He, thus, conceded the field to the smooth, articulate Chennault, who insisted that the airlift over the "Hump" concentrate on supporting the air forces. Consequently, Stilwell's Chinese forces received second call on scarce military resources. Returning to the Far East, Stilwell proved unable to cooperate harmoniously with British leaders in India. Like many experienced American leaders in this theater, he was deeply suspicious of British motives. He believed that British strategy was designed to promote prewar British Imperial power. Moreover, Stilwell lost faith in Chiang. He blamed the Chinese leader for promoting inefficiency and corruption and for retaining his forces to fight the Communists instead of the Japanese. His frustrations led to open conflict with Chiang, whom he disdainfully nicknamed "Peanut." To compound these problems, the Cairo Conference in November 1943 ended Allied plans for a major offensive in China. Thus, it was very hard for Stilwell to amass supplies to support sustained ground action. Nonetheless, by the end of 1943, Stilwell began his long-planned campaign to capture northern Burma. Its objective was the communications center at Myitkyina. Stilwell supervised an imaginative but grueling campaign that finally secured Myitkyina on August 3, 1944. By that time, Allied grand strategy had relegated Burma to a subsidiary role.

For this and subsequent offensives, Stilwell mostly relied upon Chinese soldiers. Erratic guidance from Nationalist Chinese headquarters impaired operations and led Stilwell into further political difficulties with Chiang. Finally, Stilwell appealed to Marshall, who drafted a virtual ultimatum to Chiang, signed by Roosevelt, demanding that Chiang place Stilwell in charge of all Chinese forces. Chiang called Washington's bluff. He correctly guessed that Roosevelt had too many other matters to attend to and would not force a showdown. Chiang said that he was willing to yield command to an American advisor, but not to Stilwell. The senior American diplomat in China informed Roosevelt that the main cause of all difficulties was a personality clash between Stilwell and Chiang. Accordingly, on October 18, 1944, Roosevelt informed Chiang that Stilwell would be recalled.

General Walter Krueger. Krueger's slow progress toward Manila irritated MacArthur. MacArthur sent a message criticizing "the noticeable lack of drive and aggressive initiative." Krueger refused to be influenced by MacArthur's desire to capture Manila quickly. Krueger wrote that MacArthur "refrained from directing me... to take a risk I considered unjustified with the forces available to me at the time." In spite of this dispute, MacArthur seemed to value Krueger's meticulous approach to war. When General Marshall prepared his list of first promotions to full general, Walter Krueger, who was older than the generals serving in Europe, was first on the list. (The George C. Marshall Research Library, Lexington, VA)

The pity for Stilwell was that his recall came at a time when all of his strenuous efforts to bring military supplies to Chiang were starting to produce results. Stilwell returned to the United States as chief of army ground forces, a post he kept from January to May 1945. Here, he began a long-overdue reform of the infantry replacement system. Until now, the system had relied upon individual replacements, to the detriment of *ésprit de corps.* Using his knowledge of what impeded and what assisted the making of a good combat soldier, Stilwell devised a well-conceived system that, from the moment of induction into the service, kept replacements together in small units with assignments to specific combat divisions. Stilwell's last wartime assignment was the command of the 10th Army in Okinawa. This was training for the invasion of Japan when the war ended. The next year, Stilwell died of cancer.

Among American wartime leaders, "Vinegar Joe" Stilwell was unique. He combined formidable intellectual powers, and an appreciation of language and culture, with a professional soldier's toughness. The assessment of one military historian rings true: he "might have become a great combat commander had he not been condemned to waste most of the war entangled in the political coils" of China.

Walter Krueger

Walter Krueger was born in Flatow, West Prussia in 1881. His family immigrated to the United States when he was eight years old. Loyalty to his new country caused Krueger to leave high school to enlist in the American Army and fight in the Spanish-American War. He rose from private to lieutenant. He stayed in the army and performed a variety of command, staff, and academic roles. The outbreak of World War Two found him with the rank of lieutenant-general. Assignment to training duties dashed his hopes for a combat assignment until January 1943, when MacArthur chose him to command the newly formed 6th Army in the Southwest Pacific. Krueger was 62 years old.

Krueger discovered that the 6th Army was demoralized and in poor shape, scattered over several thousand miles. He applied his training skills to restoring its fighting efficiency. Krueger's forces initially took part in MacArthur's plan to advance upon the mighty Japanese base of Rabaul. Krueger's performance pleased MacArthur, who selected him to conduct the invasion of Leyte. For the invasion, Krueger's 6th Army swelled to six divisions. His forces outnumbered the defenders by about two to one. In addition, he enjoyed nearly complete command of the air. At first, the 6th Army made rapid progress. The Japanese hoped to make their stand in the rugged mountains near Ormoc. Had Krueger advanced aggressively, his army would have captured the heights before they were well defended. Instead, Krueger committed sizeable forces to defending against a possible Japanese seaborne attack. This mistake, a "disastrous decision" according to a recent modern history, allowed the Japanese to occupy the heights in force and lengthened the campaign unnecessarily.

After the tough campaign on Leyte, Krueger led the battle for Luzon. Here, he fell afoul of his boss because he refused to accelerate the drive on Manila, which would have satisfied MacArthur's personal desire to capture the capital. Still, MacArthur again selected Krueger to lead the projected invasion of the Japanese island of Kyushu. Service under MacArthur meant that Krueger received little publicity during the war. He planned meticulously and used his forces with care. Critics complained about his caution but there was no denying that he had led the 6th Army to victory in 21 major engagements. Krueger retired from the army in 1946. He died in 1967, taking to the grave his well-earned reputation as "a soldier's soldier."

USAAF

Henry Harley Arnold

Born in 1886 in Gladwyne, Pennsylvania, Henry "Hap" Arnold graduated from West Point in 1907 and entered the infantry. In 1911, he transferred to the Signal Corps' aeronautical section and received flight training from the Wright brothers themselves. He obtained his pilot's license very quickly, thus becoming one of the first American military aviators. In 1912, he set a world altitude record and won a high aviation honor, the Mackay trophy. Arnold did not see combat in World War One and ended the war as a captain.

On December 7, 1941 the US Army Air Force had some 1,100 combat-ready aircraft. Under "Hap" Arnold's leadership, by 1944 this force had swelled to 16 separate air forces deployed throughout the world, with almost 80,000 aircraft. (The George C. Marshall Research Library, Lexington, VA)

After serving in a variety of staff positions, including several involved with public relations, in 1931 Arnold received orders to transform a training base in California into a fully operational military base. This assignment gave Arnold an opportunity to display his full range of skills. He experimented with tactics, intensified pilot training, and worked closely with scientists from the California Institute of Technology to develop new materials. Three years later, he won his second Mackay trophy for commanding a flight of ten bombers that completed a round trip flight from Washington, DC, to Alaska.

In 1936, Arnold became assistant chief of the US Army Air Corps. Two years later, he rose to major-general and became chief of the corps, which was redesignated the US Army Air Force in 1941. Although he held a variety of titles thereafter, in essence, from this date until 1946, Arnold was in charge of the American Air Force. His management and public relations experience served Arnold well during the furious bureaucratic struggles in Washington, DC. He was a strong advocate of more funding to increase the air corps' size and combat readiness. He persuaded

Arnold (left) and Marshall (right) disagreed about a great deal. Still, Arnold was determined to support the army in the way he judged best. In preparation for the Normandy invasion, the 8th Air Force, based in England, had the job of gaining air superiority. "Destroy the Enemy Air Force wherever you find them, in the air, on the ground and in the factories," Arnold ordered. (National Archives)

industrialists to modernize manufacturing processes in order to build more planes. Arnold also accelerated pilot training and pushed hard to create more private flying schools. With war drawing nearer, in 1941 Arnold managed to convince Congress to spend 2.1 billion dollars on aircraft production.

In August 1941, Arnold accompanied President Roosevelt to the Atlantic Conference. Here, he met British air leaders and began a close relationship that continued throughout the war. For the war's duration, Arnold would attend virtually every important strategic conference. In the autumn of 1941, Arnold joined the British-US Combined Chiefs of Staff as well as the US Joint Chiefs of Staff (JCS). With these prestigious assignments came promotion to lieutenant-general. Within the army chain of command, Arnold served as deputy to General George Marshall. However, he sat as an equal on the JCS. Consequently, he was able to develop a large, efficient staff to support his positions during his frequent disagreements with JCS members. Throughout the war, inter-service rivalry and Arnold's ambition to create an independent air service often rose to the surface during debates over strategic planning.

Arnold believed in the dominance of strategic bombing as articulated by theorists such as Giulio Douhet, "Billy" Mitchell, and Hugh Trenchard. A war plan he prepared in September 1941 provided the foundation for the air war logistics and strategy used in the great bombing campaigns against Germany and Japan. Arnold steadfastly focused his efforts on strategic air power, sometimes to the detriment of the overall American war effort. For example, at a time when the forces on Guadalcanal were badly in need of all possible support, Arnold resisted navy appeals for help. He suspected that it was a navy ruse to claim more resources for the Pacific. Instead, Arnold wanted all attention focused on building up forces in England to begin the massive aerial bombardment of Germany.

After the capture of Guadalcanal, planners debated how best to continue the offensive. Again, the army and MacArthur quarreled with

1: General G. Marshall
2: General D. Eisenhower
3: General Lesley J. McNair
4: War Department General Staff Identification Badge

A

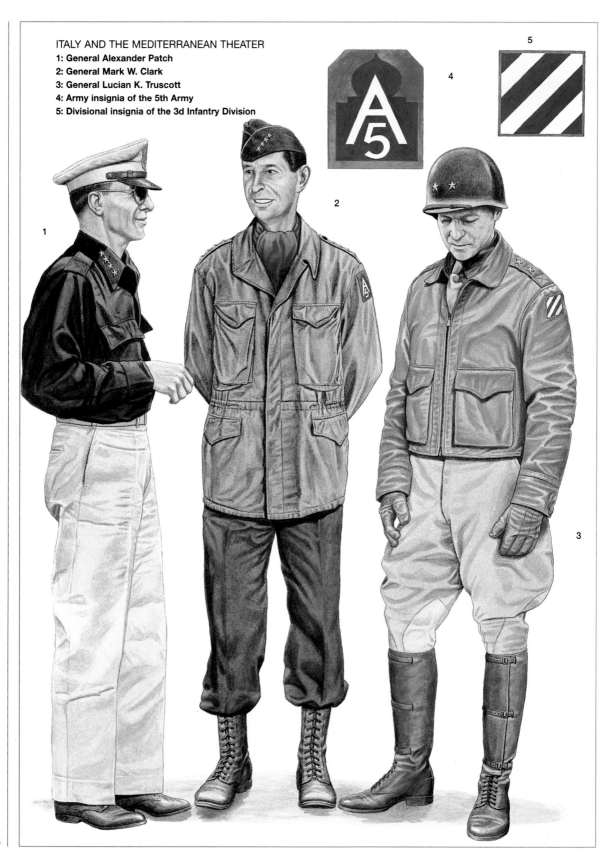

ITALY AND THE MEDITERRANEAN THEATER
1: General Alexander Patch
2: General Mark W. Clark
3: General Lucian K. Truscott
4: Army insignia of the 5th Army
5: Divisional insignia of the 3d Infantry Division

B

1: General E. Quesada
2: General Carl Spaatz
3: General C. Chennault
4–9: See text for details

C

THE NORMANDY LANDINGS
1: General Norman "Dutch" Cota
2: General Theodore Roosevelt Jr
3: General Omar N. Bradley
4: Congressional Medal of Honor

D

1: General L. Collins
2: General Wood
3: General George S. Patton

ALLIED AIRBORNE
OPERATIONS
1: General Maxwell Taylor
2: General Matthew Ridgway
3: General James Gavin
4: Parachute Jump
   Qualification Wings

F

1: General A. McAuliffe
2: General C. Hodges
3: General W. Simpson
4: European-African-Middle Eastern
   Campaign Medal
5: See text for details

G

THE PACIFIC THEATER
1: General Curtis E. LeMay
2: General Douglas MacArthur
3: General Joseph "Vinegar Joe" Stilwell
4: General of the Army five-star rank insignia

H

the navy. Both wanted the support of heavy bombers. Arnold wanted most of these still scarce planes sent to Europe. He also observed that the bombers in the Pacific were not being wisely used. As early as September 1942, he cogently commented, "It becomes more and more apparent that until there is one command, one plan, one thinking head, we will continue to misuse and hold idle our air force and our army."

In April 1944, Arnold finally obtained the combat position he desired. He became commander of the 20th Air Force in the Pacific. Although he retained his other duties and spent most of his time in Washington, DC, he personally directed the 20th's strategic bombing of Japan. Because he believed that conventional aerial bombardment could alone defeat Japan, and because this victory would enhance air force prestige enormously, Arnold opposed the use of the atomic bomb. He and Admiral Leahy were the only high-ranking officers to do so.

Arnold became general of the army, a five-star rank, in December 1944. Plagued by a heart condition throughout the war, Arnold retired in early 1946 and died in 1950. Although Arnold badly wanted an independent air service, he patriotically deferred fully promoting this goal too much until the war was over. Still, the effort to position the air service so that it could achieve independence colored Arnold's actions. In view of the fact that Arnold led a force that began the war with only a handful of modern aircraft and ended the war with the greatest air force in the world, he is remembered as the "Father of the US Air Force."

In August 1941, the US Air War Plans Division created a doctrine for strategic air power that identified three elements of an enemy's economy as key targets: petroleum, electric power, and transportation. Carl Spaatz was a strong advocate for strategic bombing. In 1944, he identified Germany's great economic weakness, oil. A mere 14 plants produced 80 percent of Germany's synthetic oil. Spaatz believed that raids against these sites, coupled with raids against Rumanian oil refineries, could rapidly and effectively curtail Germany's military power. Eisenhower thought very highly of Spaatz and recommended him for first promotion to full general's rank. Spaatz received this promotion on March 11, 1945. (National Archives)

Carl Spaatz

Born in Boyertown, Pennsylvania, in 1891, Carl Spaatz graduated from the US Military Academy in 1914. During his cadet days he acquired the nickname "Tooey." He became one of the army's first pilots and was a member of the 1st Aero Squadron, which flew in support of the Pershing Punitive Expedition to Mexico in 1916. This involved exceptional risk by flying "canvas-and-bamboo contraptions" through mountain thermals and shifting winds. Promoted to captain, he commanded the 31st Aero Squadron in France in 1917. Because he was one of a handful of experienced American pilots, he was given the duty of organizing and commanding a flying school in England. He successfully clamored for a combat opportunity and flew combat missions for three weeks. He shot down three German airplanes and once narrowly avoided death when two Fokkers got on his tail. After the war, he remained in the military. In 1927, as part of a publicity campaign to draw attention to military aviation, he was a member of a team, which included Captain Ira Eaker and Lieutenant Elwood Quesada, that achieved a flight endurance world record.

He admired General "Billy" Mitchell, the most vocal advocate for air power in the United States, and testified in Mitchell's defense during his

As one historian notes, "… in his Oil Plan Spaatz had indeed struck the touchstone of victory through air power. But no one could be sure of this in early 1944, when the airmen had already offered so many unkept promises." "Tooey" Spaatz, on right, with "Jimmy" Doolittle. (The George C. Marshall Research Library, Lexington, VA)

court-martial for criticizing existing aviation policies. This unpopular act kept Spaatz stuck at the rank of major for 15 years. Finally, in 1935, he received another promotion and graduated the next year from the prestigious Command and General Staff College at Fort Leavenworth. His big opportunity came in July 1941, when he received appointment as chief of staff to General "Hap" Arnold. Henceforth, Spaatz became one of the prime movers behind the American air campaign in Europe.

In May 1942, Spaatz became commander of the US 8th Air Force. As a disciple of "Billy" Mitchell, he strongly believed in the American doctrine of daylight, precision bombing attacks. A well-publicized, successful first raid by 12 B-17 bombers against Rouen, France seemed to vindicate the doctrine. It soon became apparent, however, that daylight bombers required fighter escorts. In their absence, Spaatz considered taking a colossal gamble: an unescorted raid deep into Germany to bomb fighter factories. Fortunately, before such a raid could be planned, strategic attention switched to North Africa. As head of Air Force Combat Command, Spaatz assumed command of the Allied air forces involved in Operation Torch, the invasion of North Africa. His ability to cooperate with British leaders led to his return to Europe in 1944 as a lieutenant-general in command of US Strategic Air Forces. He quickly fell afoul of the head of the Royal Air Force Bomber Command, Arthur Harris. Spaatz believed in the American approach of "pinpoint" bombing of selected targets, based on careful study of the enemy's economy. In particular, Spaatz wanted to concentrate on the German transportation system and oil production sites. Harris, in contrast, favored area bombing of German cities. The only point of agreement between Spaatz and Harris was the belief that air power alone could obviate the need for major ground campaigns. Spaatz's desire to leap beyond traditional army and navy objectives to destroy key elements of the enemy's economy constantly came into conflict with Allied leaders. His strategic forces were repeatedly diverted for ancillary efforts, such as bombing the U-boat pens to reduce the German submarine menace. On March 5, 1944 Spaatz presented General Eisenhower with an "Oil Plan" to cripple the German war effort but more direct support for the Normandy invasion received top priority. The summer of 1944 finally witnessed the intense bombing of oil targets. These raids dramatically reduced the German ability to wage war.

Following Germany's surrender, Spaatz went to the Pacific, where he directed the strategic air bombardment of Japan. After the war, he followed "Hap" Arnold as chief of the US Army Air Force. Spaatz lived an unremarkable retirement, beginning in 1948, until his death in 1974.

To the war's end, Spaatz remained a true believer in the war-winning potential of strategic air power. He was also one of the few senior leaders who thought in classic strategic terms. As befitting his Pennsylvania Dutch upbringing, he was patient and persistent rather than bold and brilliant.

General Lewis Brereton in France in July 1944. At that time, Brereton was still basking in the success of the June 6 airborne assault. (The George C. Marshall Research Library, Lexington, VA)

Lewis Hyde Brereton

Born in Pittsburgh, Pennsylvania in 1890, Lewis Brereton graduated from the US Naval Academy in 1911. He resigned his commission to transfer to the Coast Artillery Corps. Thereafter, he transferred to the aviation section of the Army Signal Corps to begin a career associated with military aviation. He commanded the second American observation squadron to operate in France during World War One. He rose steadily and emerged from the war as Chief of Staff Air Service for the American Group of Armies. The interwar years saw Brereton attend the Command and General Staff School and, later, serve as an instructor for four years at this prestigious institution. Brereton commanded the 17th Bomb Wing from 1939 to 1941. He rose to major-general and assumed command of Far East Air Forces based in the Philippines.

In this capacity, he became caught up in one of

World War Two's great controversies. As soon as Brereton learned that Pearl Harbor had been attacked, he pressed for permission to launch B-17 strikes against Japanese bases in Formosa. General Douglas MacArthur's autocratic chief of staff, General Richard Sutherland, refused to even allow him to talk with MacArthur. A catastrophic delay ensued. During the subsequent raid on Clark Field, dubbed the "Little Pearl Harbor," the Japanese destroyed 16 of the 18 B-17s and 55 P-40s on the ground. A Japanese pilot marveled at how Brereton's B-17s were on the ground, "squatted there like sitting ducks." How this transpired has never been explained, since the three principals, Brereton, Sutherland, and MacArthur, provided conflicting accounts. With few aircraft of the Far East Air Force left in the Philippines, on December 24, MacArthur ordered Brereton to go to Australia. Brereton offered to stay on but MacArthur believed that he could be more useful elsewhere. Brereton departed that day aboard a PBY and rejoined his surviving B-17s at Batchelor Field near Darwin. Thereafter, he served as Commander-in-Chief of Allied Air Forces Far East, where he was involved in the hopeless defense of Indonesia.

Brereton transferred to India to organize the 10th Air Force for operations in the China-Burma-India Theater. This assignment lasted until March 1942. After duty in the Middle East, Brereton returned to prominence as commanding general of the 9th Air Force in October 1943. The 9th's ragtag collection of airplanes supported Montgomery's 8th Army in North Africa. Next, it joined forces with heavy B-24 Liberator bombers for a daring, low level strike against the Rumanian oil refineries at Ploesti. By launching from desert bases around Benghazi, the target was just within the bombers' maximum range. Allied intelligence had badly underestimated Ploesti's defenses. The result was disastrous: 53 Liberators were shot down, 55 suffered severe damage, only 33 of the 178 sent on the mission were able to fly the next day. The 9th Air Force lost 579 aircrew killed, wounded, and captured.

In spite of his involvement in two notable disasters, because of his experience with directing tactical air forces, Brereton received an important new command in October 1943, a reorganized 9th Air Force based in England. The 9th was intended as a tactical air force with the mission of preparing the way for the invasion of France so it was freshly equipped with the latest models: P-38, P-47, and P-51 fighters as well as swift medium bombers and paratroop-carrying C-47 transports. By D-Day, the 9th numbered 60,000 men with 11 medium bomber and 18 fighter groups. The 9th's particular assignment was to attack enemy airfields within 130 miles of the Normandy invasion beaches. The 9th Air Force's slashing attacks first achieved air superiority and then proceeded to help isolate the battlefield by attacking transportation hubs, bridges, and trains. The contentious and flagging Allied Transportation Plan inspired Brereton to concentrate his medium bombers and fighter bombers against the Seine River bridges. By D-Day, all nine Seine bridges west of Paris had been severed. Along with General Quesada's fighter-bombers, the 9th Air Force managed to isolate the Normandy battlefield so effectively that German reinforcements were able to reach it only after a slow and painful march.

Promoted to the rank of lieutenant-general, Brereton took over command of the 1st Allied Airborne Army in April 1944. In this capacity, he helped direct the successful Normandy operations and then supervised a third debacle, Operation Market Garden. At this time, senior Allied leaders, most particularly General "Hap" Arnold, were casting about for a role for the well-rested Allied airborne forces. After a series of planned operations were canceled because of the speed of the ground advance, planners finally decided to use the 1st Allied Airborne Army in a series of drops extending to the Dutch town of Arnhem. The operation failed dramatically. Brereton provided a self-serving assessment of Operation Market Garden by placing the blame on the British 2nd Army for failing to advance with sufficient vigor and speed. He continued in command of the 1st Allied Airborne Army until the war's end. Brereton retired in 1948 and died in 1967.

Brereton's colleagues found him "perpetually discontented and querulous." His involvement in some of the war's notable debacles must reflect discreditably upon his command ability.

Claire Lee Chennault

Born in 1893 in Commerce, Texas, the son of a farmer, Claire Chennault applied to both West Point and Annapolis. Both rejected him. During World War One, he repeatedly applied for flight training but failed. He taught himself flying and earned a fighter pilot's rating in 1919. The next year, he received a first lieutenant's commission in the US Army Air Service. Thereafter, he served as a fighter pilot, commander of a pursuit squadron, instructor, operations officer, and director of training. All of this experience would prove useful during his service in China. While at the Air Corps Tactical School, he organized an aerobatic exhibition team that was the parent of the US Air Force Thunderbirds. Chennault also

Claire Chennault displayed a youthful interest in military affairs. He lied about his age to army recruiters in order to be accepted into the military. He was born in 1893 but claimed 1890 and maintained this claim for the rest of his life. (National Archives)

explored the intellectual side of air power and wrote a book that challenged the idea that strategic bombers would be supreme. He retired from the Air Corps in 1937.

Shortly thereafter, Chennault accepted an invitation from Madame Chiang Kai-shek to travel to China to survey the Chinese air force. It proved a fateful journey. Three months later, he became a personal adviser to the Chinese Generalissimo. Chennault recruited Americans to train the Chinese. In 1940, he returned to the United States to drum up support for Chiang Kai-shek's air force and to procure pilots and planes for an American mercenary air unit. The support of the China lobby and President Roosevelt overcame the objections of "Hap" Arnold. Chennault recruited 100 pilots and purchased the Curtis-Wright P-40B pursuit plane.

Chennault formed his recruits into the American Volunteer Group (AVG), composed of aircrew and ground support personnel who had been released from the US service in order to serve in China. Chennault's drive overcame daunting obstacles. His planes achieved marked success in aerial combat. Thereafter, they helped keep the Burma Road open and stopped the Japanese invasion of Yunnan Province in southern China.

Chennault enjoyed excellent press relations both because of his colorful personality and because of his superb public relations team. The press, in turn, influenced leaders in Washington, DC, to be favorably disposed to some of Chennault's wilder notions. For example, in 1942 he sent Roosevelt a plan "to accomplish the downfall of Japan" within one year, if he received 105 fighters, 30 medium, and 12 heavy bombers. Chennault claimed that he would use these planes first to destroy Japan's air force, then her shipping, and finally "destroy the principal industrial centers of Japan." Washington supported Chennault's exalted notions. Roosevelt gave Chennault command of an independent air force, the 14th Air Force. Chennault was still not satisfied. He was engaged in a bitter fight with General Joseph Stilwell (the two men hated one another) over invaluable supplies that transport planes delivered from India. To resolve the dispute, in April 1943, Chennault went to Washington, DC, to participate in strategic planning. He proved a smooth, articulate planner, in contrast to Stilwell's sullen behavior. Consequently, Chennault secured first call on scarce military resources.

Nonetheless, logistical constraints severely hampered American air power in China. To supplement regular flights by transport planes, Chennault's B-24s had to fly over the "Hump" (Himalayas) from India to bring their own fuel to their China bases. Nonetheless, during the ensuing months, the 14th Air Force inflicted serious damage against the Japanese Air Force but failed to establish air superiority. However, Chennault's advance bases in east China could not be maintained in the face of frequent Japanese bombing. Moreover, as Stilwell predicted, Chennault's bases were vulnerable to Japanese ground attack. "Ichigo," a

series of Japanese ground offensives in China, began in April 1944. Among the Japanese objectives were Chennault's bases in east China. Chennault had promised Generalissimo Chiang Kai-shek that the 14th Air Force could stop the Japanese. Although Chennault's aircrew provided skillful support to the Chinese armies, the enemy attacks could not be contained. Chennault frantically tried to persuade Chiang to divert resources from other areas. This interfered with Stilwell's operations. An angry Stilwell urged that Chennault be relieved but Washington was unwilling to dismiss a popular leader during a crisis.

Chennault had made many enemies, including "Hap" Arnold, who was suspicious of his unorthodox style. Top War Department planners, including George Marshall, did not like the way Chennault used his connections with Chiang and Roosevelt to outflank the normal chain of command. With Chiang discredited and Roosevelt dead, the way was clear to dismiss Chennault just a few weeks before the war ended. Chennault returned home, sick and bitter.

Chennault's great Far East adventure did not end with the war's termination. He remained a staunch anti-Communist and organized the Civil Air Transport, a civilian air force that provided logistical support for anti-Communist forces throughout the Far East. It became one of the world's largest air cargo carriers and served the Central Intelligence Agency. Chennault died in 1958.

For all his flaws, Chennault had shown fighting courage and brilliant improvisational skills during the early part of the war. At times, his men had been all that prevented Japanese victory over the Chinese.

James Harold Doolittle

Born in Alameda, California in 1896, James "Jimmy" Doolittle did not attend military schools. Instead, he received his education at California

Doolittle was intimately involved in air campaigns in Europe and the Pacific. He was present on the decks of the *Missouri* at the surrender ceremony on September 2, 1945. "Jimmy" Doolittle (right) and George Patton. (National Archives)

General "Hap" Arnold later described the raid on Tokyo as "nearly suicidal" and attributed its success to the "technically brilliant" flying performed by Doolittle and his men. Doolittle (on left) in 1942. (National Archives)

Lieutenant-Colonel James Doolittle pins a Japanese medal to a bomb that will be dropped by his B-25s on Tokyo. Doolittle's leadership inspired his men to overcome technical challenges. Neither Doolittle nor his pilots had ever flown a B-25 from a carrier. There was only four feet of clearance between the bombers' wing tips and the carrier's island structure. When a Japanese patrol boat detected the carrier task force, the bombers had to launch prematurely from a greater distance than had been planned. Rough seas complicated takeoff. (US Naval Historical Center)

public schools and graduated from the University of California School of Mines in 1917. He enlisted in the army during World War One and became an expert aviator and flight instructor. He remained in the Army Air Corps after the war. The army sent him to the Massachusetts Institute of Technology for advanced studies. Doolittle earned an engineering doctorate in 1925. For the next five years, he worked as a designer and test pilot. He resigned in 1930 to take charge of the Shell Oil Company's aviation department. Two years later, he set a world speed record. During the interwar years, he also served as an aviation consultant to the government and the military. The outbreak of World War Two brought this distinguished flyer and aeronautical engineer back into active service.

President Roosevelt wanted a bombing raid on the Japanese homeland. Short-range naval aircraft could not do the job at this time so 16 army bombers, modified B-25B Mitchells, were used. General "Hap" Arnold selected Lieutenant-Colonel Doolittle, who was on his staff at this time, to serve as the army coordinator for this operation. In spite of his age, 45, Doolittle secured permission to lead the raid. On April 18, 1942, Doolittle flew the first B-25 from the deck of the carrier *Hornet* to attack Japan. The bombers inflicted minor damage and continued to China, where the air crews bailed out or crash-landed. A postwar US Naval War College study determined that there was "no serious strategical reason" for this raid. Yet, it had an enormous impact on Japanese planners. It served as the catalyst for the Japanese to accelerate plans to attack Midway Island. Because he knew that the bombers had inflicted minimal damage, Doolittle expected to be court-martialed for failure. Instead, he returned a hero, was promoted two ranks to brigadier-general, and received the Congressional Medal of Honor for leading this morale-boosting raid.

A plume rises more than 60,000 feet above Nagasaki on August 9, 1945. General Doolittle assessed the role of the strategic bombing campaign against Japan and the use of the atomic bomb: "The navy had the transport to make the invasion of Japan possible, the ground forces had the power to make it possible, and the B-29 made it unnecessary." (National Archives)

Promoted again to major-general, Doolittle assumed command of the 12th Air Force in support of Operation Torch, the invasion of North Africa. Doolittle's leadership then, and thereafter, while supporting the invasions of Sicily and Salerno, impressed General Eisenhower. When Eisenhower took charge of Operation Overlord, he requested that Doolittle join him in England. Accordingly, Doolittle took command of the 8th Air Force. In March 1944, he became a lieutenant-general and received an honorary Knight Commander, Order of the Bath from King George VI. The 8th's role was to help prepare the way for the cross-channel attack. When, in early March, Doolittle visited the 8th Fighter Command, a unit assigned to bomber escort, he saw the unit's motto on a sign: "Our Mission is to Bring the Bombers Back." Doolittle ordered the sign taken down. "From now on that no longer holds," he explained. "Your mission is to destroy the German Air Force." The ensuing air war over Germany became a grim battle of attrition. Doolittle deliberately chose targets that he knew would compel the

MacArthur's army air force had been unable to assist effectively the ground offensive against Buna in New Guinea. It was near useless against ships at sea. MacArthur had lost confidence in the air commander, so in August 1942, George Kenney assumed air command. (National Archives)

German planes to take to the air to defend them. Fierce aerial battles raged but Doolittle knew that his forces could afford the losses and that the Germans could not.

Doolittle retired from the Air Force in 1946. He returned to the Shell Oil Company, while continuing to fill many advisory slots in both the public and private sectors. He retired from business in 1959 and died in 1993. He was one of America's great aviators.

George Churchill Kenney

Born in Yarmouth, Nova Scotia, in 1889, George Kenney grew up in Boston. He attended the Massachusetts Institute of Technology and became a civil engineer. He served as an army pilot in World War One, shot down two enemy aircraft, and earned several awards for bravery. He remained in the army after the war, serving as an instructor, test pilot, commander, and staff officer. Pearl Harbor found Brigadier-General Kenney commanding the Air Corps Experimental Depot.

Promoted to major-general, Kenney arrived in Australia in July 1942. He found a demoralized, inefficient air organization. Kenney made major personnel changes, dismissing five generals within his first two weeks. Unfit colonels and majors soon followed. In their place, Kenney installed aggressive, capable flyers. Soon, the planes began to perform better and helped to isolate the Japanese garrisons in Papua New Guinea. Kenney believed that air superiority was a prerequisite for air, ground, and sea operations.

Kenney also won an all-important battle for command control against MacArthur's domineering chief of staff, Richard Sutherland. When Sutherland tried to overmaster Kenney, Kenney grabbed a blank piece of white paper. He drew one small black dot in the corner and then said to Sutherland, "The blank area represents what I know about air matters and the dot represents what you know." Sutherland recognized that he had met his match and allowed Kenney the command latitude he needed and, most importantly, unrestricted access to MacArthur.

Kenney quickly understood the role of air power in the Pacific. He wrote to General Arnold, giving a summary of the situation: "In the Pacific we have a number of islands garrisoned by small forces. These islands are nothing more or less than aerodromes or aerodrome areas from which modern fire-power is launched. The Air Force is the spearhead of the Allied attacks in the Southwest Pacific. Its function is to clear the air, wreck the enemy's land installations, destroy his supply system, and give close support to troops advancing on the ground."

Kenney's greatest contributions came shortly afterwards. He researched why army bombers had performed so poorly against ships and concluded that they attacked from too high an altitude. He ordered experiments with low-level attacks. Through the fall and winter of 1942–43, army aircraft practiced attacks against an old wrecked ship off

Port Moresby at altitudes as low as 150 feet. When a major Japanese convoy, carrying reinforcements to New Guinea, appeared off the western tip of New Britain Island, Kenney's new tactics had a trial. One hundred aircraft, including 30 specially modified B-25 bombers, sank eight transports and four destroyers during the March 1943 Battle of the Bismark Sea. Three thousand Japanese soldiers perished. Fifteen years after General "Billy" Mitchell had predicted the ascendancy of air power, Kenney's airmen demonstrated that air power was the dominant weapon in the Southwest Pacific. MacArthur based his subsequent strategy of bypassing Japanese strongholds in New Guinea on Kenney's ability to gain air superiority, isolate the enemy, protect Allied forces, and provide close air support. Kenney recognized the important role played by the air force's ground support teams. He worked hard to boost morale among these teams. In addition, he proved to be a skilled logistician.

Kenney also contributed his talents by influencing strategic planning. He traveled to Washington, DC, to attend planning sessions for the offensive against Rabaul. MacArthur wanted more heavy bombers for this offensive. The air force leaders wanted all the heavy bombers sent to Europe. In the past, planners almost always endorsed the notions supported by their own branch of the service. At this meeting, Kenney supported his boss, MacArthur, over the objections of the air force leaders.

MacArthur's subsequent drive to the Philippines took place beyond the range of Kenney's planes. Until airfields could be built on Leyte for the army air forces, MacArthur had to rely upon naval aviation. Kenney and his staff blundered seriously when they discounted concerns expressed by engineers regarding the difficulty of building bases in the Philippines. It was one of the few blemishes on Kenney's wartime record.

Kenney emerged from the war with a well-deserved reputation as an innovative leader capable of successfully tackling wide-ranging

The five feet, six inches tall George Kenney combined scrappy tenacity with technical brilliance. His innovations included low level bombing tactics against ships. One of the bombs used was the parafrag, a 23lb fragmentation bomb with a small parachute so that the bomb could be released from low altitude and the bomber still have time to escape before explosion. The parafrag worked very effectively against aircraft on the ground. Another Kenney innovation, 100lb incendiary bombs, were dubbed "Kenney cocktails." Kenney shares a light with Douglas MacArthur. (The George C. Marshall Research Library, Lexington, VA)

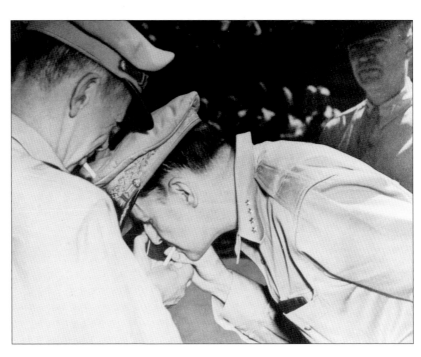

By all accounts, Curtis LeMay was an odd individual. He "was a big, husky, healthy, rather stocky, full-faced man... He apparently couldn't make himself heard even in a small room except when you bent all your ears in his direction, and when you did, he appeared to evade your attempt to hear him. He did this by interposing a cigar or pipe among which words were trying to escape through teeth which had obviously been prised open only with an effort, an effort with which the speaker had no real sympathy." However, there was no denying his great military talents. (National Archives)

problems. After the war, he commanded the Strategic Air Command from April 1946 to October 1948. Upon retirement, he wrote his wartime memoirs and two biographical books about notable American wartime pilots. He died in 1977.

Kenney deserves high marks for his wartime leadership. He developed a strategy during his first campaign in New Guinea and did not deviate from it: gain air superiority and use air power to isolate the battle area; on the day of the invasion concentrate everything on supporting and protecting the invasion force.

Curtis Emerson LeMay

Born in Columbus, Ohio, in 1906, LeMay left college to enlist in the National Guard as a flight cadet. He received his pilot's wings in 1929 and joined a fighter squadron. After completing a civil engineering degree, he transferred to bombers because he believed that bombers were more likely than fighters to have a decisive impact in any future war. He quickly became known as the best navigator in the air force. In 1937 and 1938 he was the lead navigator on two mass B-17 demonstration flights. LeMay was a major on December 7, 1941. The following May he took command of a bombardment group that was slotted to be the first unit to enter the European war. He proved a driven and demanding leader, earning the nickname "Iron Ass."

LeMay brought the 305th Bombardment Group to Britain in the autumn of 1942. At this time, bombers typically flew evasive patterns while trying to drop their bombs. He brought mathematical modeling to bear to challenge the prevailing wisdom that stated that any bomber in a combat zone that flew straight for more than ten seconds would be shot down. To prove his point, he led an attack, during which he flew a straight course for seven minutes until he released his bombs. His new technique soon became standard practice. LeMay also designed a formation that massed 18 bombers in such a way that defensive fire could cover all angles.

In June 1943, LeMay assumed command of the 8th Air Force's 3rd Bombardment Division. On August 17, 1943, LeMay led one of the war's most famous missions, the "shuttle mission" that took off from Britain, raided Regensburg, and landed in North Africa. For his personal heroism, leadership, and innovative tactics, LeMay received promotion to brigadier-general in September 1943 and major-general in March 1944. He was just 37 years old. In August of that year, he transferred to the China-Burma-India Theater.

At the beginning of 1944, the only bases within B-29 range of Japan were in China. The Joint Chiefs created a new organization, the 20th Air Force, to direct the B-29s. Yet, logistical problems kept the B-29s from operating efficiently. To fuel one B-29 for one raid required six transport planes loaded with fuel to fly over the "Hump" from India to bases in

China. Moreover, they were experiencing teething problems. LeMay observed that, "cylinder heads often blew out the moment an engine started turning over, ignition was faulty, oil leaked excessively, fuel transfer systems gave endless trouble." The combination of equipment malfunction and fuel shortage kept the B-29s from flying more than an average of two missions per month. The performance of the 20th Air Force angered General Arnold. He ordered LeMay to take charge.

LeMay quickly improved performance by ordering practice missions against poorly defended targets and increasing the size of the basic bomber formation. However, results remained less than spectacular. Then came a change in December 1944. While supporting a Chinese ground offensive against Hankow, Formosa, the B-29s dropped incendiaries, including the most advanced type, a gelatinous slow-burning gasoline called napalm. The Hankow raid destroyed most of the city's docks and warehouses. Still, logistical problems made strategic bombing from China too difficult. LeMay recalled, "About four missions a month was the best we could do out of China, and sometimes we didn't even manage that." Consequently, attention shifted to bombing from offshore islands.

A 1943 photograph taken from a B-17 belonging to LeMay's 8th Air Force during a raid against a ball-bearing plant in Paris. (National Archives)

The Joint Chiefs created the 21st Bomber Command to operate from Saipan, Tinian, and Guam. This command experienced the same teething problems that had plagued the 20th Air Force. High winds and clouds also hampered the raids. General Arnold decided to make changes to improve effectiveness. In January 1945, LeMay relieved the commander of the 21st Bomber Command. Even the dynamic LeMay could not improve the bombers' accuracy from high altitude. By early 1945, it was clear that daylight precision bombing, as delivered by B-29s, was not particularly effective. American strategists had long been aware of the potential vulnerability of Japanese cities to fire attack. Therefore, attention turned to the notion of using the B-29s to carry incendiaries instead of explosive bombs. On February 4, 1945, LeMay's bombers exclusively dropped incendiaries on Japan's sixth-largest city, Kobe. The attack seemed effective so LeMay ordered a similar raid against Tokyo on February 25. Some 28,000 structures burned to the ground; a square mile of the city was destroyed. Bad weather had forced the B-29s about 5,000 feet lower than usual. When he looked at bomb assessment photographs, LeMay concluded that the lower bombing altitude had helped. After conferring with Washington, he authorized a change in tactics that represented a radical departure from the long-held tenets of daylight precision bombing. LeMay decided that low level, night-time, saturation fire raids should replace precision bombing. Such an approach would have failed against German defenses but LeMay showed that he could adjust his tactics according to the situation. Early in March, an American flyer guided his B-29 on a test flight over Tokyo. The plane returned without damage. LeMay concluded, "I think we can do it." Moreover, LeMay took responsibility for the outcome.

B-29s were prepared for this special operation by removing everything extraneous, including their machine-gun ammunition, so that they could carry more bombs. LeMay ordered his disbelieving pilots to attack singly rather than in formation. In March 1945, over 330 bombers, armed exclusively with incendiaries, struck Tokyo in a low level raid. Some 267,000 buildings burned to the ground, and more than 83,000 civilians perished. The destruction of Tokyo was arguably one of the greatest single disasters in military history. LeMay immediately understood the raid's significance. He reported to General Arnold, "the destruction of Japan's ability to wage war lies within the capability of this command." The Tokyo raid set the pattern for the remainder of the war. LeMay's force increased to over 600 bombers. They flew virtually unchallenged over their targets and gutted Japan's most important cities. When not dropping fire bombs, they dropped aerial mines that shut down Japanese coastal traffic through the Inland Sea.

By mid-June 1945, LeMay's photo interpreters reported that all of Japan's larger cities, except for those reserved as demonstration cities for the atomic bomb, had been burned out. Attention shifted to fire-bombing smaller cities while other bomber formations attacked selected industrial targets. It still appeared that a direct invasion of Japan would be required. To direct the massive air effort, in August, General Spaatz arrived to assume command of the US Strategic Air Forces in the Pacific. LeMay became his chief of staff. LeMay played a major role in planning the atomic attacks against Hiroshima and Nagasaki.

After the war, he commanded the US Air Force in Europe, the Berlin airlift in 1948–49, and then the Strategic Air Command (SAC). In this capacity, he served as the architect of US strategic air power and formed SAC into the Cold War's ultimate nuclear strike force. In 1951, he became the youngest four-star general in American history since Ulysses Grant. Vilified both for his support of the Vietnam War and participation in the atomic bomb attacks against Japan, LeMay was ridiculed in later life as a "caricature of the ultimate cold warrior." He died in 1990.

LeMay was one of America's most influential military commanders during World War Two. General Spaatz called him one of the war's greatest air combat commanders. His decision to switch the B-29 tactics in the raids against Japan has been described as one of "the most momentous decisions in modern warfare."

Elwood Richard Quesada

Born in Washington, DC in 1904, Elwood "Pete" Quesada did not attend the nation's military academies. He showed an early interest in flying, received a commission in the Air Reserve in 1925, and began active duty in 1927. Ira Eaker and Carl Spaatz selected First Lieutenant Quesada in 1929 to join them in an aerial refueling trial, which set a world record with more than 150 hours of continuous flight. During the interwar years, Quesada held a variety of flying and high-level staff assignments. He helped create the organization for the Army Air Corps' new general headquarters staff and designed the criteria for the lend-lease shipments of aircraft and munitions to Great Britain. In these assignments, he honed his communication and organizational skills.

"Pete" Quesada's successful efforts to link mobile ground forces with tactical air support were a key element in the American breakout from Normandy. General Omar Bradley commented, "This man Quesada is a jewel." (National Archives)

Holding the rank of brigadier-general, Quesada went to North Africa in 1943 to command the 12th Fighter Command. His assignment was to impede Axis shipping and protect Allied convoys. He transferred to England to take charge of the 9th Fighter Command, received promotion to major-general, and then assumed command of the 9th Tactical Air Command. This position called upon his organizational and training skills as the 9th Tactical Air Command prepared to support the Normandy invasion. In spite of years of training in England, the Allies had not worked out a flexible, fast response method for tactical air support. Quesada arrived in France on June 18 and immediately went to work overcoming organizational problems and, more importantly, obstacles posed by faulty doctrine. He established his headquarters adjacent to General Bradley's headquarters so that the two staffs could work closely together. He piloted his own P-38 fighter from airfield to airfield to explain his tactics and motivate his men. Bradley told Quesada, "Your airmen reflect your enthusiasm."

Quite simply, Quesada wanted to give ground forces the best support possible, regardless of all else. He ignored Royal Air Force (RAF) protests and shocked airmen by converting Britain's best fighter, the Spitfire, into a fighter-bomber. "But they're not your planes any more," he told RAF leaders, "they're mine. And I'll do anything I want to with them." He persuaded Bradley to give him a Sherman tank so that he could experiment with ground-to-air liaison. Dissatisfied with the available AM radios, he sent a sergeant back to New York to buy very high frequency ground (FM) radio equipment. He installed the equipment in the tank to demonstrate how tanks could effectively communicate with close-support aircraft. Soon, this equipment became standard. Quesada's efforts reached fruition during Operation Cobra, which opened on July 25, 1944.

At this time, the 9th Tactical Air Command had 12 fighter-bomber groups based in France. Quesada's orders stated in part: "Each of the rapidly advancing columns will be covered at all times by a four ship flight... [which] will maintain a close armed recce in advance" of the column. Coordination between the 9th Tactical Air Command and the ground forces worked brilliantly, as Bradley's tank columns first broke through the front lines and then exploited the success, to unravel the German position in Normandy. Bradley reported to General "Hap" Arnold, "Quesada was a peach to work with, because he was not only willing to try everything that would help us, but he inspired his whole command with this desire to such an extent that these youngsters now do almost the impossible whenever they think we need help."

Quesada continued to hone close support tactics. A new challenge came during the Germans' Ardennes offensive in December 1944. To overcome bad weather and poor visibility, Quesada helped develop a blind bombing technique that worked remarkably well. Then, when clear weather returned, his fighter-bombers dominated the battlefield.

Quesada's planes, like this rocket-armed P-47, acted as armed aerial scouts for the fast-moving tank columns during the Normandy breakout. If the target required more than the four-ship flight, the combat commander on the ground could call upon additional fighter-bombers, which were armed and ready for takeoff just a short distance behind the front lines. (National Air & Space Museum)

Field Marshal Montgomery with the two American combat leaders he most respected: "Lightning Joe" Collins (left), the best US corps commander of World War Two, and airborne commander Matt Ridgway (right). (National Archives)

After the war, Quesada became the first commander of the Tactical Air Command and served as the military director for the first hydrogen bomb tests. He retired in 1951 to establish the Missile and Space Division at Lockheed. In 1959, he became the first administrator of the newly formed Federal Aviation Administration. He died in 1993.

Quesada was an innovative thinker and tireless worker. He focused on problem solving and, far more than most officers, overcame inter-service rivalries. The foremost tactical air commander of the war, Quesada "was one of the architects of the modern tactical air support system for ground combat operations."

BIBLIOGRAPHY

Ancell, R. Manning and Miller, Christine M, *The Biographical Dictionary of World War II Generals and Flag Officers,* Westport, CT: Greenwood Press, 1996

Costello, John, *The Pacific War 1941–1945,* New York: Quill, 1981

Dear, I.C.B., ed. *The Oxford Companion to World War II*, New York: Oxford University Press, 1995

Jablonski, Edward, *America in the Air War,* Alexandria, VA: Time-Life Books, 1982

Polmar, Norman and Allen, Thomas B, *World War II: America at War 1941–1945,* New York: Random House, 1991

Sandler, Stanley, ed., *World War II in the Pacific: An Encyclopedia*, New York: Garland Publishing, 2001

Weigley, Russell F, *Eisenhower's Lieutenants*, Bloomington: Indiana University Press, 1981

Zabecki, David T, ed., *World War II in Europe: An Encyclopedia.* 2 vols. New York: Garland Publishing, 1999

THE PLATES

A1: General G. Marshall

General Marshall is wearing an olive drab service dress tunic with white shirt and black tie, along with light tan elastique trousers. By 1942, the white shirt and black tie combination was replaced for all occasions by an olive drab shirt and tie. The olive drab coat and tan trousers were referred to as "Greens and Pinks," the green referring to the olive drab of the coat and the pink referring to the tan of the trousers, which had a somewhat pinkish cast. The gold buttons with a heraldic eagle and the US insignia on the collar are those worn by all army officers, but generals, who routinely commanded personnel of multiple branches, did not wear branch of service insignia. In common for all officers, rank insignia, in this case four stars, is worn on the shoulder straps, and the olive drab worsted lace stripes on both lower sleeves are the same as for all officers, $5/8$ inch in width. General Marshall wears the optional M1923 officer's leather belt with cross strap; this belt was replaced in late 1942 with a belt made of the same material as the coat, which closed with a flat, square brass buckle.

A2: General D. Eisenhower

General Eisenhower is shown in the outfit he wore on the eve of the Normandy invasion. He wears an olive drab side hat; piped in gold cord, rank insignia on the left side. Illustrated is the M1927 officer's short overcoat, with an olive drab scarf. The short overcoat was a popular alternative to the officer's long overcoat, both of which had the same black mohair braid reserved for general officers; other officers had no decoration on the cuffless sleeve. The officer's overcoat was made up of heavy moleskin wool in a light fawn color, with green sateen lining. The buttons were horn or Bakelite in a light brown color, and the coat had a belt of the same material, fastened by two coat buttons. The M1927 coat can be distinguished from the new model instituted in 1943, which featured notched rather than shawl lapels, and had adjustment straps and buttons on the lower cuff.

A3: General Lesley J. McNair

General McNair wears the forerunner of the "Ike jacket," the ETO (European Theater of Operations) jacket. This jacket has the same cut as the M1941 field jacket, but since they were both intended as a service dress items, each was made up of olive drab woolen material with brown composition buttons. In 1942 and 1943, this uniform was very popular with several generals, including Eisenhower and Spaatz, who even had a tropical khaki ETO outfit.

A4: War Department General Staff Identification Badge

This special identification was authorized for wear by all officers of the US Army who had served as members of the War Department. The badge was to be worn on the right side of all uniform jackets, centered on the breast pocket.

B: ITALY AND THE MEDITERRANEAN THEATER

B1: General Alexander Patch

General Patch was the commander of the United States 7th Division, tasked with the invasion of southern France following the Normandy landings. The General is shown in a variation of the shirtsleeves dress often worn by officers in warm climates. He wears the dark OD smooth gabardine open-collared shirt with rank insignia and shoulder loops and two external breast pockets with button flaps. The general's chino trousers are of a light shade of khaki similar to the British khaki drill.

B2: General Mark W. Clark

General Clark, the commander of the 5th Army, and later the 15th Army Group, shows a more standard appearance in his choice of uniforms in this print. Clark is outfitted with the M1943 pattern field jacket that the general was instrumental in having secured as standard combat issue for American soldiers. Made of olive drab (OD) cotton canvas duck material, the M1943 was found to be an improvement over the M1938 "Parsons field jacket," which it replaced. Soldiers in combat found that the M1943 was a superior product

George Marshall possessed the essential talent of picking good subordinates. Omar Bradley appears fourth from the left, then Joseph Stilwell, George Marshall, George Patton, Terry Allen, and Theodore Roosevelt Jr. Allen commanded the 1st Infantry Division, and Roosevelt was one of the heroes of Omaha Beach. (The George C. Marshall Research Library, Lexington, VA)

"Ike" Eisenhower sees the paratroopers load for departure on June 5. General Bedell Smith recalled that the toughest moment Eisenhower faced was watching the 101st Airborne prepare for departure, because the British Air Marshal, Leigh-Mallory had confidently told Eisenhower to expect the division to suffer 80 percent casualties. (National Archives)

because they had access to the pockets of the garment while wearing full combat gear.

The most unusual feature of General Clark's uniform is the addition of a blue silk neck scarf worn in the manner of an ascot. Many of General Clark's staff officers wore these scarves due to the general's affection for them; blue was the color of choice because of Clark's affiliation with the infantry, and it being the infantry's color.

B3: General Lucian K. Truscott
General Truscott was commander of the 3d Infantry Division and, subsequently, the 5th Army. His uniform shows the great deal of latitude that American generals had in wearing individualistic clothing during time of war. Truscott wears a private purchase aviator-style jacket, similar in configuration to the USAAF's A-2 pattern, and brown leather gloves. The general's uniform is completed with a pair of officer's "Pink" riding breeches, brown leather three-buckle field boots and a standard issue M-1 steel helmet.

B4: Army insignia of the 5th Army
The 5th was activated in French Morocco in January 1943; hence, the distinctive blue mosque on the patch. The 5th holds the distinction of having the most days of continuous combat (602) of any contemporary United States Army.

B5: Divisional insignia of the 3d Infantry Division
Nicknamed the "Rock of the Marne," this division served in the Southern Theater of Operations throughout World War Two. One of the most notable members of this division was Audie Murphy of the 15th Infantry Regiment, one of the most decorated US soldier of World War Two.

C1: General E. Quesada
General Quesada wears the summer khaki wool service dress uniform, with khaki shirt and tie, which items could be either wool or cotton. The service dress coat bore the same

insignia and was of the same cut as the olive drab winter service tunic, with two exceptions: there was no cloth self-belt and no gussets ("bellows") in the back, so prominent a feature of the olive drab coat. Generals Spaatz, Quesada, and Chennault had all been awarded the Distinguished Flying Cross (C7), the pre-eminent award for airmen. Medals were worn only for full dress occasions such as parades and other specified occasions, while only the ribbon representing the medal was worn for ordinary duties. It should also be noted that the wearing of ribbons was not under ordinary circumstances mandatory, and many veterans chose to wear only some, or none, of the ribbons to which they were entitled. Qualification badges, however, were always to be worn, not only on coats but also on shirts when coats were not worn.

C2: General Carl Spaatz
General Spaatz also wears a khaki service dress coat of tropical weight wool with matching straight trousers. On his upper left sleeve he wears the patch indicating his former unit affiliation, in this case the 8th Air Force (C5). (C4) shows Gen. Spaatz' ribbon array. The awards in order from left to right are, top: the Distinguished Service Cross and the Distinguished Service Medal; second row: the Legion of Merit, Silver Star, Bronze Star, Mexican service medal; third row: World War One victory medal, American Defense Medal, Europe Africa and the East Campaign ribbon, Asiatic and Pacific Campaign ribbon and The American Campaign ribbon.

C3: General C. Chennault
General Chennault wears the olive drab service uniform coat and illustrates the method of wear of several unusual features. Over his right breast pocket, the general wears the Nationalist Chinese pilot's badge, commemorating his service with the American Volunteer Group ("Flying Tigers") in China. General Chennault wears on his upper right sleeve the

After his 5th Army captured Rome, Clark wanted to pursue vigorously. To his frustration, Allied planners had different priorities. In a 1944 scene in Italy, Clark stands third from left. (National Archives)

Chennault's American Volunteer Group (AVG) developed tremendous *ésprit de corps* and became known as the "Flying Tigers" because of the large sharks' teeth painted on their planes' noses. Their P-40s were inferior to Japanese aircraft. They lacked decent radios, gun sights, bomb racks, and auxiliary fuel tanks. However, Chennault trained his aircrew relentlessly in tactics that he had personally developed. Chennault's tactics avoided dog-fighting with Japanese planes. They took advantage of the P-40's diving ability, instead, so that pairs of planes conducted fast, hit and run attacks in order to negate the superior Japanese maneuverability. During the six months following Pearl Harbor, the AVG downed nine Japanese planes for every one it lost. (National Archives)

patch of the 15th Air Force (**C6**), the successor organization to the American Volunteer Group. On his left upper sleeve can be seen the China-Burma-India Theatre patch (**C9**) as his current unit affiliation. The general wears his ribbons in a non-regulation manner, with fewer ribbons in the lower than in the upper row. To the left of the China-Burma-India patch is the so-called "Blood Chit" (**C8**) – obscured here originated again by the AVG. This patch varied, sometimes showing US and Chinese flags, sometimes only one, but all contained Chinese text naming the wearer as a US pilot and requesting aid from the populace. The chit was worn on the flight jacket, usually on the back, by aircrew flying over Chinese territory.

D: THE NORMANDY LANDINGS
D1: General Norman "Dutch" Cota
General Cota was deputy commander of the 29th Infantry

Division. His uniform is based on the standard combat infantryman's gear in 1944. The general, being part of the assault divisions to land on Omaha Beach, is wearing the navy issue M1926 inflatable life ring, designed to allow for increased mobility for the troops, rather than the standard "Mae West" life vest, which was common at the time for other services. The rest of General Cota's gear is: the M1941 pattern field jacket known as the "Parsons jacket" after its designer General Parsons; woolen combat trousers in an early war characteristic light OD tan canvas; M1938 gaiters; M1941 army issue ankle boots also known as "low quarters," and a model M-1 steel helmet.

D2: General Theodore Roosevelt Jr
General Roosevelt, deputy commander of the 4th Infantry Division, was the only American general to arrive with the first wave of the assaulting troops. Once described by a

contemporary as "the most disreputable looking General that he ever met," Roosevelt was well known for his rough and ready appearance as a soldier. The general had a distinct dislike of the steel helmet, so was often to be seen wearing the knitted wool OD jeep cap, as pictured in the plate. Roosevelt's uniform is the same as the common infantryman's, with tall canvas gaiters over the short brown leather ankle boots, wool OD trousers, M1941 "Parsons jacket" and canvas web gear consisting of a pistol belt, ammo pouch and brown leather .45 holster. One unusual feature of Roosevelt's uniform is the addition of a heavy wooden walking stick with metal spike base.

D3: General Omar N. Bradley
General Bradley, commander of the US 1st Army, who was nicknamed the "GI" general by war correspondent Ernie Pyle, in many ways typifies the businesslike look affected by many US commanders during World War Two. Bradley's uniform consists of the standard wool OD shirt and combat trousers in a darker shade of material more common to the latter war period. The general also wears the two-buckle combat boots that began to replace the low quarters and gaiters by 1943. Finally, Bradley's one concession to the general's prerogative to individualized uniforms is the addition of the M1938 "Tanker's jacket," characterized by its external zipper and knitted collar and cuffs and waistband.

D4: Congressional Medal of Honor
The Congressional Medal of Honor is the highest award for bravery in the United States service. This medal was won by General Theodore Roosevelt for his actions on June 6, 1944. "Under his seasoned, precise, calm and unfaltering leadership, assault troops reduced beach strong points and rapidly moved inland with minimum casualties. He thus contributed substantially to the successful establishment of the beachhead in France."

E1: General L. Collins
In this illustration, General Collins presents a typical US general in the informal and comfortable field uniform derided by his German adversaries as "golf clothing." The general uses a field telephone and wears a woolen "Tanker's jacket" with knitted collar and cuffs and, like General Patton, wears dark olive drab combat trousers and standard field boots. His unit patch is that of the 4th Armored Division, which he commanded in 1944. His cap is the so-called "overseas" cap in dark olive drab elastique wool. This cap was standard for all army officers, except for the solid gold cord piping on the curtain, which replaced the mixed gold and black cord worn by officers below general officer rank. General Collins stands before a Dodge command car equipped with a fold-down tailgate for use as a field table.

E2: General Wood
General Wood also wears the popular "Tanker's jacket" of light olive drab wool, but in addition wears a light olive drab wooled shirt with matching tie. On the points of his shirt collar he wears the insignia of his grade, two silver metal stars, identical to those worn on the left side of his dark olive drab overseas cap. His unit patch, worn in a more conventional position than that of General Collins, is that of the 4th Armored Division.

E3: General George S. Patton
General Patton wears the trench coat introduced in 1942. This coat, in conjunction with the M1943 field jacket, was intended to replace the old woolen overcoat. As it was not available in sufficient quantities, its wartime use was largely limited to officers. The trench coat was made of waterproofed cotton sateen, and featured a blanket wool button-in liner. It had light brown composition buttons and a cloth belt with a square composition buckle. General Patton has a 3d Army patch on the upper left sleeve, and over the coat wears a black leather non-regulation belt and holster housing an ivory-handled M1873 Colt revolver (on the right-hand side – obscured here). The trousers are the dark olive drab woolen trousers, worn with standard two-buckle brown boots. The general's helmet is the standard helmet introduced in 1942, decorated with three silver stars on the front.

F: ALLIED AIRBORNE OPERATIONS
F1: General Maxwell Taylor
General Taylor, commander of the 101st Airborne Division, is pictured as he looked prior to the Allied airdrop in Holland. He wears the M1943 field jacket and M-1 steel helmet, with its paratroop-style medical pack attached to the general's helmet net. General Taylor is geared up for his jump, with a parachute (white stripes) with a quick-release device attached.

F2: General Matthew Ridgway
General Ridgway, commander of the 82d Airborne Division and later the XVIII Airborne Corps, is pictured wearing the USAAF A-2 leather flying jacket favored by many officers of the 82d Airborne. The general's A-2 jacket has an 82d Airborne Division patch on the breast, underneath his leather nametag, and the twin stars of a major-general on his shoulder straps. Ridgway's headgear is the dark OD garrison cap with gold piping and two silver rank stars.

F3: General James Gavin
General "Slim Jim" Gavin, commander of the 82d Airborne Division, was one of the US Army's youngest combat commanders of World War Two. Shown here in the uniform that he wore during the Arnhem Operation Market Garden, General Gavin wears the model M1942 paratroop jacket with its characteristic slanted breast pockets, two-button cuffs, cloth waist belt, and central back gusset. The trousers are the matching M1942 pattern with large side pockets closed by two buttons. General Gavin, being a combat general, wears the standard M1910/36 series pistol belt. General Gavin is armed with an M-1 Garand rifle rather than the lighter carbine.

F4: Parachute Jump Qualification Wings
These wings were awarded to any personnel who had completed the prescribed training at the airborne school or had participated in one combat jump. Jump wings were issued in grades of Basic, Senior and Master parachutist, according to the number of jumps made. Unofficially, during World War Two, combat jumps were recorded by the addition of bronze stars to the wings.

G1: General A. McAuliffe
General McAuliffe is wearing the B-15 jacket issued to aircrew and normally associated with the army air forces. This waist-length coat was made of sage green nylon, fastened with a zipper, and had a synthetic brown pile collar. The waist and cuffs had ribbing for warmth. General McAuliffe's helmet is not the airborne model but is, rather, the general issue helmet, with white-painted divisional artillery insignia. **G5** shows the general's unit affiliation, the famous "Screaming Eagle" of the 101st Airborne Division.

Bradley (left), Eisenhower, and Patton in Bastogne on February 5, 1945. Montgomery's claim of credit for saving the situation in the Ardennes infuriated Bradley. (National Archives)

BELOW William Simpson (right) rides in a staff car with George Marshall . Simpson's professionalism was emulated by his staff, who worked with painstaking attention to detail and accomplished their missions w quiet competence. Simpson was dependable and his superiors, particularly Omar Bradley, grew to like and trust him. (The George C. Marshall Research Library, Lexington, VA)

This device was not only worn on the upper left sleeve of shirts, coats, jackets, and overcoats; it was also, not uncommonly, painted on the side of the helmet.

G2: General C. Hodges

General Hodges wears another form of the "Ike jacket," this one in dark olive drab elastique. As the fashion grew for short uniform jackets, such as the ETO and later the official "Ike jacket," many officers modified their existing service dress coats by having the skirts cut off in imitation of the "Ike jacket." Like the regulation jacket from which it was made, this improvised jacket retained the exposed gold uniform buttons. These jackets were worn routinely with both the dark olive drab and the tan elastique trousers.

G3: General W. Simpson

General Simpson wears the so-called "Ike jacket" with the medium shade olive drab shirt and a light olive drab (khaki) tie. Shirts worn by US officers varied from a dark olive drab shade, best described as chocolate brown, to a light khaki color. The tie was to be a light khaki color. The waist length "Ike jacket," derived from the 1940 British battle dress, was intended to be issued to all ranks as a combat uniform. However, insufficient quantities were produced during the war, so the uniform was worn almost exclusively by officers until very late in the war. These uniforms were made up in an enlisted style cloth, rough serge in a medium olive drab color. General Simpson's status as a combat commander is indicated by the dark green underlay on his shoulder straps.

G4: European-African-Middle Eastern Campaign Medal

The European-African-Middle Eastern Campaign Medal was authorized by the Executive order of President Roosevelt in November 1942. It commemorates the service of all branches of the US military during the conflict in this area. (December 7, 1941–November 8, 1945)

H: THE PACIFIC THEATER

H1: General Curtis E. LeMay

General LeMay's uniform is the typical dress for officers

serving in the Pacific while not in front line combat situations. It consists of a khaki chino shirt and trousers. The general's cap is the tropical version of the service cap, with a khaki chino cover and brown leather bill and chin strap. The general's rank insignia is worn on the collar of his shirt and, due to his status as a pilot, General LeMay wears his command pilot wings over the pocket flap of his shirt.

H2: General Douglas MacArthur

General MacArthur was Commander-in-Chief of the Army of the Philippines and, subsequently, commander of the US Army in the Pacific. He was the pre-war commander of American and Philippine forces based on the Philippine archipelago. Due to the tropical climate, uniforms for service in the Pacific were often of a lighter shade and weight of material than the temperate versions of service dress. General MacArthur is shown in a pre-war white dress uniform, similar in cut to the service dress coat, with a white shirt, black tie and white buckskin shoes. The insignia worn on the left breast pocket of the general's tunic is the War Department General Staff Identification badge. This identification was authorized "for optional wear by officers of the United States, who, since June 4, 1920 have served not less than one year as regular or additional members of the War Department General staff." Of particular interest is the general's distinctive headgear. MacArthur was appointed Generalissimo of the Philippine Army so the service cap, with its heavy gold wreath embroidery, is of that rank and station.

H3: General Joseph "Vinegar Joe" Stilwell

General Stilwell, commander of the China-Burma-India Theater, is shown in his frontline uniform, consisting of the M1941 field jacket and OD trousers with tan gaiters and boots prescribed for field service. Stilwell's main eccentricity in dress is the addition of the M1912 "Campaign" hat with the distinctive Montana peak to its crown. The general's version of this headgear has a set of gold hat cords with acorn ends to distinguish his rank.

H4: General of the Army five-star rank insignia

This was established by Congress in December 1944 to recognize the achievements of the supreme US Army commanders. The silver stars, arranged so as to form a pentagon in their center, were worn on the shoulder straps of the service jacket, along with a miniature US eagle crest.

MacArthur, wearing sunglasses at front, preparing for a radio broadcast upon his return to the Philippines. During subsequent operations on Luzon, MacArthur put heavy pressure on his subordinates to seize Manila quickly. He told the commander of the 1st Cavalry Division, "Go to Manila, go around the Nips, bounce off the Nips, but go to Manila." There was no sound military justification. One of MacArthur's subordinates believed the haste was due to MacArthur's desire to capture Manila before his birthday. Likewise, MacArthur ordered his forces to liberate the entire Philippine archipelago even though this effort was not part of the strategy devised by the Joint Chiefs of Staff. He embarked upon this campaign, to redeem his pledge to free the Philippines, at the expense of sound strategic judgment. (National Archives)

INDEX

Figures in **bold** refer to illustrations

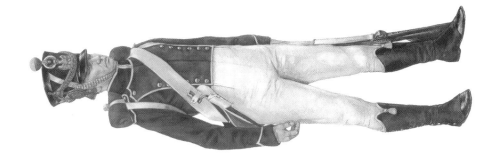

FIND OUT MORE ABOUT OSPREY

❏ Please send me the latest listing of Osprey's publications

❏ I would like to subscribe to Osprey's e-mail newsletter

Title/rank

Name

Address

Postcode/zip   state/country

e-mail

I am interested in:

❏ Ancient world
❏ Medieval world
❏ 16th century
❏ 17th century
❏ 18th century
❏ Napoleonic
❏ 19th century

❏ American Civil War
❏ World War I
❏ World War II
❏ Modern warfare
❏ Military aviation
❏ Naval warfare

Please send to:

USA & Canada:
Osprey Direct USA, c/o MBI Publishing, P.O. Box 1, 729 Prospect Avenue, Osceola, WI 54020

UK, Europe and rest of world:
Osprey Direct UK, P.O. Box 140, Wellingborough, Northants, NN8 2FA, United Kingdom

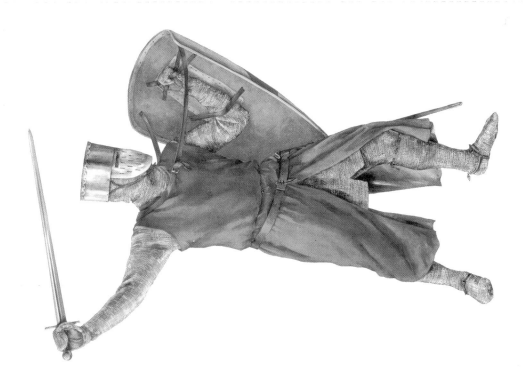

Young Guardsman
Figure taken from *Warrior 22:
Imperial Guardsman 1799–1815*
Published by Osprey
Illustrated by Richard Hook

www.ospreypublishing.com

call our telephone hotline
for a free information pack

USA & Canada: 1-800-826-6600
UK, Europe and rest of world call:
+44 (0) 1933 443 863

Knight, c.1190
Figure taken from *Warrior 1: Norman Knight 950 – 1204 AD*
Published by Osprey
Illustrated by Christa Hook

POSTCARD